LIQUID LOVER

Liquid Lover

a memoir

John Moriarty

alyson books
los angeles | new york

MANUFACTURED IN THE UNITED STATES OF AMERICA.

THIS TRADE PAPERBACK ORIGINAL IS PUBLISHED BY
ALYSON PUBLICATIONS,
P.O. BOX 4371, LOS ANGELES, CA 90078-4371.
DISTRIBUTION IN THE UNITED KINGDOM BY
TURNAROUND PUBLISHER SERVICES LTD.,
UNIT 3, OLYMPIA TRADING ESTATE, COBURG ROAD, WOOD GREEN,
LONDON N22 6TZ ENGLAND.

FIRST EDITION: JULY 2001

01 02 03 04 05 a 10 9 8 7 6 5 4 3 2 1

ISBN: 1-55583-631-3

LIBRARY OF CONGRESS CATALOGING-IN-PUBLICATION DATA
    MORIARTY, JOHN (JOHN EDWARD, 1957–
        LIQUID LOVER : A MEMOIR / BY JOHN MORIARTY.—1ST ED.
        ISBN 1-55583-631-3
        1. MORIARTY, JOHN (JOHN EDWARD), 1957–   2. GAY MEN—ALCOHOL
    USE—UNITED STATES. 3. ALCOHOLISM—UNITED STATES—CASE STUDIES.
    4. ALCOHOLICS—REHABILITATION—UNITED STATES—CASE STUDIES.
    5. RECOVERING ALCOHOLICS—UNITED STATES—BIOGRAPHY. I. TITLE.
    HV5139.M67 2001
    362.292'092—DC21
    [B]   2001022576

COVER DESIGN AND ILLUSTRATION BY MATT SAMS.

DEDICATION AND THANKS

WHEN MY MORNIN' COMES AROUND

When my mornin' comes around, no one else will be there
so I won't have to worry about what I'm supposed to say
and I alone will know that I climbed that great big mountain
and that's all that will matter when my mornin' comes around

When my mornin' comes around, I will look back on this valley
at these sidewalks and alleys where I lingered for so long
and this place where I now live will burn to ash and cinder
like some ghost I won't remember
When my mornin' comes around

When my mornin' comes around, from a new cup I'll be drinking
and for once I won't be thinking that there's something wrong
with me
and I'll wake up and find that my faults have been forgiven
When my mornin' comes around

Iris DeMent

Welcome

For nearly 40 years, the geography of my life is a liquid line that loops from one day to the next week to the following month. Mistakes and misgivings mass in the distance, an army of resentful marauders that wait out of view, reminders that I am weak, insensitive, selfish; that I thirst for escape from anything difficult, taxing, confrontational.

The years pass. High school, college, graduation, employment. I work as a writer in Kansas City and New York, producing corporate public relations materials, feature articles, ad copy. I write about the employees of a media company, artists and interior decorators, boating supplies and lawyers and pet food. I write a serial for a newspaper, another that appears on the Internet. I write letters to friends in distant cities. I write notes to myself and journal entries, paragraphs and sentences and words that capture the casual disintegration of my world.

And the years pass. Boyfriends come and go. Romance, love, disappointment circled by a steady flow of strangers who engage me in vacuous erotic encounters. Life becomes a brittle house of broken cards, erected to conceal an unbalanced and fragile ego. Questions surface. Why do I feel alone in a crowd? How can I tell my close friends about the constant metronome of anxiety that clicks softly behind my sad eyes? What happened to yesterday? To my dreams? To the future?

Years pass. I am alternately alone, elated, pensive, tired, angry. I frequently drink through the night at bars or parties, in the homes of strangers and friends, arriving at work the next morning with a hangover, fractured memories, the dull ache of dread that always accompanies the activity of drinking through the night until the rising sun signals that it is time to shower and dress for work. Always sad, rarely centered, never serene. Mistakes, misgivings, mindless sex. And always, always, always alcohol. My liquid lover, my comrade in harm.

And the years pass. Boyfriends come and go. More strangers, mistakes, failures, fears. The liquid line loops about my throat, threatening to choke the supply of air that keeps the madness beating, threatening to end this wild, weary, lurching life.

I exist in this desert of aimlessness and drought as the years pass like identical periods of pleasure and pain, an unbroken chain of unfulfilled dreams, a massive sprawl of ambition. There is no control, no center, no plan for a productive and fruitful future. I move without meaning, speak without consideration, vault over objections from friends and family that my life is not working and I should consider seeking clarity, honesty, truth. There is no direction, only imperfect intentions without release, life without hope.

And then, it all changes.

It all changes and I am reborn.

It all changes and I create a second life, something that was once a dream and has now become reality.

It all changes on a Tuesday in April. On a Tuesday night during the fourth month of the year, I experience a miracle. It is a simple and small moment in time, the kind of thing that most people dismiss as a common occurrence, the kind of thing that would attract little or no attention. I understand the reaction; some miracles are monumental in size, others are barely detectable. Some break the surface to shatter the silence, others hum quietly just beneath the radar, sending a wave of enlightenment, harmony, and love into the universe.

My miracle happens again and again as each new dawn sketches the sky with pastels of pink, blue, bronze, gold, and white. My miracle happened yesterday. It happened today. And as long as I honor my new life and the sobriety that guides me, it will happen again tomorrow.

My miracle is not unique. It has happened for thousands of men and women before me and will fill thousands more with hope, inspiration, and direction in the days ahead. To begin the story of my miracle, I invite you inside one recent night, a Tuesday night in April, a Tuesday when friends celebrated their miracles in separate and distinct ways. From a dinner party in New York to an anxious single mother in Massachusetts and from a couple moving into their first home to a man who surrenders to his addiction, the events of this Tuesday night are a simple portrait of sobriety's power.

It is a monumental day. The first day I stand before a group of fellow survivors and speak my truth aloud. The first day I finally establish a link between dreaming a miracle and living one. The first day I am proud to acknowledge the events of my past as I embrace the pleasure of the present and move forward into the promise of the future.

So welcome to the story of one man's miracle. If you seek a similar experience, I wish you luck and peace. If you seek understanding of another's struggle with addiction, I wish you patience and understanding. When we join our hearts and spirits, we provide a bridge between the chaos of addiction and the serenity of sobriety to every man and woman who desires to make the journey through the darkness and into the light.

———

Angels arrive when we need them, when we are ready for miracles, when we are ready for dreams to come true. Some angels are messengers, others are guardians and guides. In the first three years of my new life, I meet many angels. Each is a blessing, an aspect of the miracle—a thread in the rope that connects hope to humanity, truth to integrity, wisdom to the heart.

———

The group gathers in a painter's loft near downtown Kansas City on a Tuesday night in April. It's the same Tuesday night that Riley celebrates his 32nd birthday with a feast at Florent in New York's West Village. The same Tuesday that Anna leaves for a week in San Francisco, that Clark starts a new job in Chicago, that Graham calls to tell me he's checking into a clinic in Minnesota to conquer his cocaine addiction.

It's a Tuesday night in April, the second week of the month, the week that Chad and Eliot are moving into their new house, the week that Sara quits her job in Boston and moves to the Berkshires, the week that I learn to stand in front of my fellow survivors and say the phrase I once muttered in disgust and now say with pride and honor.

"Hello," I say to the group. "My name is John, and I am an alcoholic."

The other occupants of the room, some glancing at their hands, others drawing deep breaths through their burning cigarettes, look up and say, "Hi, John!"

The room is silent, a hushed space sprinkled with anticipation, patience, a warm and embracing love. From Baltimore Street, six blocks down and a world away, I can hear random cars passing in the night, a distant horn, a dull hum of cars on the nearby interstate. The metallic sound of a train moving toward Union Station floats like tin flakes through the air, clinging to the shadows, climbing on the breeze.

I look around the room and continue. "This is the first anniversary of my sobriety," I say, "and I thank you for letting me share my story with you. It's taken me a very long time to speak about these things. I used to be ashamed of the truth, but I've learned a lot in the past year. I've learned that being honest about my old life is the only way to build a foundation for my new one."

I pause, take a breath, look around the room. My friends' faces tell me they are familiar with the hesitation to talk, the shame about the truth, and the ongoing challenge to be honest about addiction and recovery. Every man in the room remembers the terror of telling the truth. Every man can provide detailed recollections of the brittle balance he maintains with faith, love, support, pride. Every man can describe his newfound confidence, the clarity that comes with time, patience, and the concentrated belief that each one of us deserves a new chance at a new life.

It feels good to speak about the details, to share my story, to listen to the experiences of my fellow travelers on the road to recovery and sobriety. The opportunity to talk honestly about our drinking is also an opportunity for closure and healing and growth. Talking honestly about addiction and recovery feels solid and true, a sturdy platform of unconditional support that I share with my fellow survivors.

Many years before I actually quit drinking—when I started talking about my alcoholism in group meetings held in public spaces or small gatherings in private homes—I excluded one significant detail. In fact, I was speaking about my alcoholism without giving an honest account of my life as an alcoholic and without including the key that linked my addiction and my recovery. During those meetings, I selectively omitted one significant detail: I'm a gay man, a gay alcoholic.

Only in the past three years of being clean and sober have I found the clarity to connect the proverbial dots that link my drinking with my sexuality. Identity is consequential to all that we do in life. It's the core of our personal lives and the collective weight of our professional pursuits. In the life of a recovered addict, identity—especially who we were then and who we are now—is the most significant measure of progress, healing, and the promise that sobriety will survive.

As I stand in the loft on a Tuesday night in April, I reflect on who I am today and who I was in the years before I quit drinking. While I once spent my evenings slipping gradually into a coma concocted of vodka—a substance I called Vitamin V—and barbiturates, I now spend time with friends and family members, enjoying and remembering dinner parties and special occasions and the mundane activities that define a life lived in pursuit of positive pleasure instead of a race away from articulate interaction and everyday human contact.

Then and now, unique characteristics, personal elements of identity. As the drinking days fade with each passing year, I'm enjoying a second chance to redefine myself and rededicate my life to sharing the love, compassion, and kindness that made it possible for me to escape the fatality of alcoholism.

Then and now, names and labels, signs of individuality. What else am I besides a gay alcoholic? Each element of our identity is added to the charm bracelet that encircles our hearts, minds, and spirits. So, in addition to being gay and an alcoholic, I'm a writer. I love to laugh. I love to walk, run, swim. And I also love chocolate. I'm a bad bowler, a fan of Joan Didion's novels and nonfiction, a patient listener, and, on occasion, an intolerant talker.

I adore my sanity and the memories that collect in my mind like orderly schoolchildren on the first day of class. I enjoy the occasional cigarette, watch movies with admiration and keen interest, spend hours talking on the telephone, and find great solace in the unconditional love and affection I share with a wide circle of wise friends.

In the days before I quit drinking and rejoined the human race, I invested countless hours in a mad dash away from reality. Today, I limit my rambling to frequent travels along the two-lane black ribbons of asphalt that divide wide open spaces of this country into irregular kingdoms, spaces captured in map books though never tamed by their place on a page.

There are so many differences between my life today and my existence during the drinking days. I used to be very good at employing falsehoods and misstated details to escape detection, to fly beneath the radar, to create a pool of opportunity in which I could wade with my liquid lover. Now the only time I lie is never.

When I was drinking, I would help only myself. I'd help myself to more liquor, I'd help myself to another excuse, I'd help myself to steer clear of real commitment or detectable human emotions. It was a selfish life, a hollow and cold tunnel of tuneless melody, blank canvas, empty promises.

Now I know how to help myself while I help others. I help myself by defining goals and objectives that are within my capabilities as well as those that challenge me to reach further and rise higher. I help myself by keeping a clear eye on a clean and healthy path. And I help myself by believing that I am forgiven for past mistakes, that I can learn from present opportunities, and that I will enjoy the rewards of my new life in the future.

I help others by listening to their fears, their stories, their hopes, their burdens. I help others by lending a hand, offering support, giving encouragement or sharing a smile when their view is obstructed by clouds and their road is difficult to see. I help others by demonstrating that it is entirely possible to shake off the shackles of addiction—to substances, emotional duplicity, negative thinking, and the other obstacles that divert our eyes and hearts from the true beauty of a temperate life.

I love life rather than a lifestyle.

I love myself rather than my selfishness.

I am honest and faithful instead of faithlessly dishonest.

In this new world, I believe in miracles. I am surrounded by angels. And I will follow my heart with faith, friendship, compassion, and courage. Sobriety is a miracle. Recovery is a blessing. I am indebted to the men and women who extended their hands and hearts when I fell, when I was in pain, when I needed love and support to extinguish the confusion and agony of alcohol's embrace and influence. It is through their guidance, advice, wisdom, and support that I found the initial strength and courage to regain my place in the world. I thank them, and I honor their strength and courage by passing along the love and support to other spirits who seek redemption and recovery.

If there's one word that describes my experiences in the past three years, it is this: Believe.

And I do.

1 / FREE

I am dead.

I am alive.

Suspended between the two, I'm pulled by fear and anxiety and loneliness into a self-medicated spiral of alcohol and sex. Alcohol creates a cocoon of comfort and familiarity, a protective covering to deflect pain, grief, insecurity. Sex is a safe haven, a transparent shelter crafted from artificial images of myself and the mumbled affections of men I meet in bars, on the street, at parties hosted by friends. The journey that began with a young boy's curiosity about his father's beer ends 30 years later with an unshaven, soiled man crawling from his bed to the bathroom, huddled over the white porcelain toilet, staring at the black and white tiles on the floor, praying for deliverance from the chaos that had become life.

I am dead.

I am alive.

And, in the end, I am alone. I'd stumbled through a nine-month romance with Dylan, an Irish Catholic package of timidity, nurturing love, and selfish disregard. He knew my drinking history when we met. I soon learned that he straddled a deep crevice between life as a gay man and life as the son of a homophobic family. I loved him with greater clarity than I'd ever loved another man, but I sensed he would never truly commit to our relationship. He spoke frequently about his parents, but said I could never meet them. We never spent more than a few minutes at his house, staying most nights at my apartment, where he felt safe and protected—but I felt trapped and surrounded by the ghost imprints of my past mistakes, a parade of one-night stands, drunken cycles of frenetic and pointless activity.

During the months I spent with Dylan, my behavior was colored by the duplicity of drink; his actions were shaded by insecurity and a lack of confidence. The love appeared true, the bond seemed strong, but thoughts of our future made me uneasy and apprehensive, constantly needing an alcoholic veil to numb the anxiety and fear.

It was an imperfect relationship. We could both be selfish, moody, cold. I accepted, perhaps envied, his devotion to the church and his family. I loathed his closeted side and his silence whenever there was an issue that needed to be discussed. He expressed concern over my drinking, fearing that it was the only tangible threat to our happiness. I assured him it wasn't a problem, pretending the Vitamin V bottles I secretly drained on a daily basis were necessary allies in my battle against fear and depression.

In the end, I win the battle. But I lose the man. After a final four-day binge, during which I try to end my life with a voluminous blend of alcohol and barbiturates and antidepressants, I find someone else. Someone new. Someone unknown. After three fifths of Vitamin V and two packs of cigarettes and an agonizing night sprawled on the bathroom floor vomiting blood and praying for death, I lose Dylan but find myself.

It's an answered prayer, a form of deliverance, a vision of heaven.

And I know that I will never again return to the darkness. I'm alone for the first time in years, but I am also free.

Finally.

At long last. Irrevocably.

Free.

2 / LESSONS

Look at this photograph, a color snapshot taken on a Saturday morning in May, a brief moment from the early years of one man's life. In the picture, a boy relaxes on the floor of a suburban family room, wearing brown socks and white pajamas and a misshapen grin. He is 8 or 9, and his blue eyes gaze into the camera without hesitation from behind black glasses that sharpen his imperfect vision. He is happy and comfortable, lounging before a television set that fills the room with the frantic sounds of Saturday cartoons. If you draw close to the image, you can almost hear the boy laugh, the sound of someone who has not yet experienced decades of drink, failed relationships, faded friendships, his father's death, dozens of opportunities lost to his love of alcohol.

I am the boy in the photograph. A chubby child who

found security in undisturbed routines and familiar surroundings, a boy who spent endless hours with his mother and sensed nothing more than silent waves of disapproval from his father. Those weekend mornings remain among my most treasured memories, providing smooth and simple pleasure when I recall childhood's uncomplicated pace. Inside my parents' house, I was safe. I escaped emotions and experiences that seemed unsettling or difficult. I easily deflated the jealousy I felt when other boys gathered for baseball games or basketball contests. I eluded the discordant inferiority that consumed me when I was ignored or ridiculed for being shy, overweight, passive.

I was a ghost in those days, moving silently among the crowd, observing life from a distance and avoiding anything or anyone that was unfamiliar. Within two or three years of that Saturday morning in May, I discovered an unwavering ally in the battle to overcome my childhood insecurity. My ally was not a boy from the neighborhood, a nurturing parent, or an interested teacher. My partner was alcohol, a seductively powerful companion whose silent stranglehold convinced me it would provide everything I thought I lacked. Alcohol made me feel calm, it made me feel whole. In simple and complex ways, alcohol made me feel OK.

In those first encounters with my future lover, I found an instant way to momentarily mend the ache of rejection and soothe the sadness that grew from the knowledge that I wasn't just shy but was somehow truly unlike the rest of the boys in my class. I learned that alcohol could erase the feelings of insignificance that flooded my mind when peers treated me like an outsider.

At the age of 10, I came to understand that the difference I felt had nothing to do with my weight, a Boy Scouts membership, or success on the football field. The difference was my sexuality, and although at that age I couldn't give it a name or articulate its impact on my life, I knew the attraction I felt for other boys was the evil, sinful way of life I'd heard described at school, in church on Sunday, by members of my own family.

———

"Do you want some?" Julian asks. "It's good. It will make you feel big."

It's a summer afternoon, a soggy Saturday in July. We're standing among the overgrown weeds and tangled brush that chokes an abandoned farm near our neighborhood. Julian invited me to join him for a walk, suggesting that I would be less than a man if I decided not to join him. When we reached the safety of the farm, Julian opened his backpack, revealing a six-pack of chilled beer.

"Try it," he says. "It will make you feel better."

"I feel OK," I tell him. "Did you take that from your Dad?"

He smiles, the proud face of a victorious thief. "Yes," Julian says. "He'll never miss it. He has tons. My parents are having a party this weekend."

Julian is older by three years. I imagine he is smarter, more clever, less intimidated by parental admonitions. I trust him. I am 10, a studious boy who spends hours alone in his bedroom, writing and reading and dreaming. Julian and I share the fate of the misfit, ignored by most of the kids in our neighborhood, pleased to have found a friend for after school adventures, backyard camping expeditions, idle hours at the pool during summer vacation.

It takes just a few seconds beneath his harsh, coaxing gaze for me to surrender. I wrestle a beer from the plastic holder, hear the snap of the tab as it slides inside the can, watch as the foam cascades out of the opening and onto my hand. It feels cold and sticky, the first kiss from a future love.

"I knew you'd try it," Julian says, beaming with brotherly pride. "I knew you couldn't say no."

———

Here is a second image, another photograph from my life. It is 30 years after that Saturday morning in May. A pair of plaid boxer shorts and a white T-shirt have replaced my baggy pajamas. I am standing near the water's edge at Polihale Beach on Kauai beneath a brilliant, cloudless canopy that hangs high above the Hawaiian Islands. With the cliffs of the Na Pali coast at my back, I squint into the camera, an older version of the young boy in the photograph from 1965. The bulky black glasses have been replaced by contact lenses, the smile is surrounded by shallow wrinkles, the excess weight has been erased by years of dedicated exercise. You can see the same blue eyes, though they now telegraph the painful, constant conflict that consumed me in those days.

In the picture taken that afternoon on a deserted beach, the location's serenity and my smile belie the struggle I endured during the early stages of sobriety, the pain that woke me in the night and the loss that wrenched my heart. It had been two months since I survived my final, brutal binge with alcohol, two months since my boyfriend had vanished without a single word. I had traveled to Hawaii to celebrate my recovery and mark the initial days of my second chance at a sane, sober life.

There were other reasons for my presence on the lush, languid island in the Pacific. There was my need for solitude and isolation. On Kauai, I would be completely focused on the issues at hand: the reasons I drank, the reasons I betrayed myself and my boyfriend, the reasons I disappointed my family. I was confident that Kauai's tranquility would nurture my body, mind, and heart as I contemplated the lessons I faced now that I had quit drinking. On the island, among the majestic palm trees, fog-shrouded peaks, sculpted canyons, and terraced taro fields, I would accept the past, embrace the present, and plan for the future.

I traveled to Hawaii to make sense of my life, to understand my motives, to analyze and interpret the choices that had ruptured a nine-year period of recovery. With confidence and a sense of purpose, I arrived on Kauai ready to sort through the remnants of recent days and the history of my alcoholism. I expected the process to be difficult, but I never knew how hard it would be to learn the first lesson of sobriety: I could no longer douse discomfort, pain, anxiety, or any other emotion, good or bad, with alcohol.

———

"It sounds like a great trip," a friend says two weeks before I leave for Kauai, "but are you sure you should go so far from home right now?"

I smile. "Far from home is where I need to go. I've got to get out of here and think."

We're having coffee at Starbucks near my apartment. It's a Sunday afternoon in April, and the unseasonably warm spring weather has encouraged crowds of shoppers to spend the day browsing the stores and sitting in the sun. I'd agreed to meet Kirk for coffee after he phoned earlier in the day.

As always, his regular weekend call began with a detailed account of Friday night at work. Kirk is a waiter at a popular, upscale restaurant, and once a week he entertains me with stories about coworkers and patrons. When he finishes the latest installment of his saga, Kirk arrives at the question so many friends ask these days.

"How are you doing?"

I know the inquiry is coming, but it always amuses me when Kirk tries to make it sound like a casual follow-up to his report from the restaurant wars.

"Am I drinking?" I say quietly. "Isn't that what you mean?"

I don't want to sound defensive; I'm simply practicing my newfound skills of honest, direct communication. It is foreign territory, and I fumble my way through the first few weeks feeling like an immigrant who's just arrived at Ellis Island from some distant land. The surroundings are unfamiliar. Language is a challenge. The idea of fleeing back to familiar territory—in my case the life of an active alcoholic—is more attractive than this alien world.

"Yes," Kirk says. "That's what I want to know. How's it going?"

"Fine," I tell him. "I feel great. Not every day, all day, but this is my second month of clean and sober, and it feels amazing."

Kirk is in his third year of recovery. We met at an AA meeting a year earlier, two strangers who recognized each other from the bar circuit and the drunken chaos of crowded dance floors. We became fast friends, colleagues on the long, slow march to recovery. I enjoyed Kirk's attitude about alcoholism and his regular reports of new self-help books, magazine articles, or Internet postings.

Kirk was the first person at AA to encourage my return, to offer pamphlets of information, to suggest I call—day or night, local, long-distance, or collect—if I needed to talk or feared I was headed toward that first deadly drink. Although I attended meetings for several months, I continued to drink. And to lie. I told Kirk the same things I told everyone else. I was alcohol-free. I was clean. My sobriety was holding, the terror had ended. I was healing rapidly and had confidence that I would never again pick up another drink. It would be 12 months before I replaced those lies with truth, before I finally bowed out of the alcoholic waltz that kept me moving in turbulent circles through drunken days and nights.

Over coffee that afternoon before my trip to Kauai, Kirk and I discuss our disease and the lessons we're learning about sobriety. Kirk's wisdom and insight are sharp; he listens to my comments and slices through to the true message, even if I can't hear it myself. He doesn't judge or indict; he offers suggestions or alternatives when I struggle with issues and conflicts.

"You know," he says as the sun pours through the windows and warms my face, "if you drink in Hawaii, you'll be a long way from home."

I sip my latte. "Perfect," I tell him with a smile. "At least it won't be quite as public as my last relapse."

———

During my early drinking years, alcohol gave me faith that I would find my place in the world. I was ignorant then; a naïve newcomer to a world filled with deception, misery, and grief. It took decades for alcohol to destroy my most cherished relationship, threaten to end my life, and erode the confidence I had gained from years of success as a writer. Alcohol made me question the actions, intentions, and comments of close friends and family members, even strangers on the street.

Alcohol is a jealous lover, a resentful companion, an envious ally. Spend enough time in its embrace, and alcohol undermines every goal and plan. It tests your endurance, weakens your spirit, jeopardizes your sanity. Surrender to its power, and alcohol teaches you new lessons: to obey, to beg, to plead for its presence in your life.

———

Find me. I will wait. Capture my heart. I will capture yours. Take this moment to tell me one secret. Breathe this life into your soul. Angels come when we are ready.

Find me.

———

"You don't want him," the boy says to his friend. "He's fat and he runs like a girl."

The pair studies my face with contemptuous stares. We are 9 or 10, a group of boys in the school yard on an overcast afternoon. The daily drama of selecting team members during recess has begun, and I stand at the end of the line, sandwiched between two friends who share my fate as undesirable and embarrassing.

"Do you think we'll get picked?" Andy looks at the team captains as they prowl the pavement. "I hate being the last one."

"Me too," I say. "But there's nothing we can do about it."

Nothing to do but accept the truth and wait. Standing beneath the leaden sky, watching anxiously as the line of potential competitors grows smaller, I want to run, head home, escape the emptiness of knowing that I am unwanted, a nuisance who will land eventually on one squad or the other by default. At the time, I was more ashamed than hurt. I felt like everyone was watching and they knew I was a poor athlete. They knew I spent evenings and weekends as my mother's companion instead of learning the skills and sports most young boys have perfected by their teenage years.

When they reach a certain point of maturity, newborn birds are forced into the air by their parents. With fragile wings and undetermined destinations, they attempt to fend for themselves. Some fly high, others fail. When I was young, my parents did not persuade me to face the simple choices that challenge most children. I was never bitter about their lack of encouragement, but it took years to recognize that the missing pieces of my personality were the result of lessons I never learned as a child.

I never wore a Boy Scout uniform, never discovered how to send a baseball arcing into the air. While my peers developed social skills and self-confidence to deal with life on its terms, I hid within myself and held my breath, hoping that everything would somehow be resolved without my involvement.

Three decades passed before I mastered life's simple talents, before I learned to deal with everyday anxiety and disappointments. Three decades of drink, three decades of misery, three decades of deception. While most people develop these coping skills by confronting life's hardships, I began to learn them during four dark days spent alone in my apartment, a self-designed crucible of alcohol, damage, and tragedy.

———

"Can I have a sip?" I ask my father, my uncle, my brother. The question is met with a grin, a masculine wink.

"Sure," they say. "Why not?"

I feel bigger, bolder, brighter. I am one of them now, one of the adults, one of the gang. I am no longer an outsider, the misfit, the unacceptable nuisance.

"Just one sip," a voice says from across the room. It is my mother, a sister, an aunt. "Don't let him get drunk."

The remark is answered with laughter. The adults play their roles in this endless familial circus like peerless thespians. I am the novice, the lamb, the virgin. I am unfamiliar with alcohol, liquor, booze. They are the wise elders, introducing me to the pleasures of my future by allowing me to have a sip of their beer, martini, manhattan. No one suspects that they are also handing me a whip, a dagger, a dangerous ticket.

"That's enough," my father says. "You're too young for more than a taste."

I want to please him. I want to please them all. I want them to accept me, make me feel welcome, assure me that I'm OK and safe. I want them to still my anxious heart and silence the voices in my head, the voices that mumble and murmur a constant dialogue of disharmony and fear. I want to please my father, my brothers, my uncles. I want to feel like I belong in this family, that I'm accepted and loved. In some small way, I hope that participating in the ritual of alcohol and laughter, the ceremony of liquor and lies, will somehow help me connect with the world.

"Didn't you hear me?" my father says, reaching for the beer can. "I said that's enough. Now go outside and play."

———

Children learn about loss in terms of misplaced toys, windows broken by errant baseballs, childhood friends who move away without warning. Though these losses are painful at the time, they are shallow wounds that mend quickly. Untouched by experience and unblemished by remorse, young hearts heal rapidly.

But the heart of an adult faces a more consuming challenge. After multiple disappointments, years of real or perceived damage, and the wisdom that grows from repeated defeat, loss is at once an easier and far more difficult burden to bear. Toys that disappear mysteriously can be replaced. Shattered panes of glass can be mended. And the friends of youth, seemingly so important at the moment they leave, can be supplanted with new faces.

During the drinking years, I learned to find solace not in prayer or the company of friends, but in the contents of clear glass bottles, ice-filled tumblers, and the hypnotic warmth of a glass of cabernet or merlot. I anesthetized the dark moments and disappointments with drink. I was not alone. Whenever I needed to escape, my trusted companion, my friend and ally was ready to accompany me on the dark journey away from my life.

At the time, the choice to drink—though ultimately

destructive and irretrievably damaging—made sense. It was a logical action, the right thing to do. It was the only response to discouraging events, the pressures of troubled relationships, and the chaos that seemed unshakable and permanent. When I lost jobs, boyfriends, treasured possessions, or professional opportunities, I flooded the void with Vitamin V and casual sex in an attempt to find instant relief. With a stream of liquor and a long list of nameless bedmates, I erased the pain and numbed the uncertainty, blotted the stain of failure that had followed me into my adult years from its first appearance during my childhood.

———

"Will you do us a favor?" I ask the man outside the liquor store. "Will you buy us a six-pack?"

I am 13, a thirsty teenager on a Friday night. Julian, Tim, Greg, and I are standing a few feet away from the small package liquor store that adjoins a nearby motel. We have money, motive, intent. The only ingredient we need may be the man who smiles at us from behind a pair of mirrored sunglasses. It's 9:30 on a Friday night in August and he's wearing sunglasses. Somehow, the detail fits perfectly with our fraudulent goal.

"You got the money?"

I pull a pair of faded $5 bills from my pocket. He accepts the money, tips his head back, asks what brand.

"Doesn't matter," Julian says. "Just don't let the guy know it's for us."

The man lifts his sunglasses and glares at Julian. "I'm not the stupid one here," he says. "I'm old enough to buy my own beer. Why don't you babies just relax. I'll be right back."

Tim and I laugh at Julian when our conspirator disappears inside the store.

"Don't be assholes," Julian snaps. "Without me, you guys

would be home watching TV with your Mommy and Daddy."

Julian is right. I've learned a lot from him in a short period of time. I've learned how to lie. How to steal money from my father's wallet. How to drink. And how to smoke a joint.

"Sorry," I say. "We didn't mean it."

The man returns with our beer. We thank him, accept the brown paper bag, head off to the parking lot of a local discount store. We spend the next few hours drinking, talking, slipping further away from the innocence of youth.

―――

"Anything goes," the woman tells me. "I don't judge you. You don't judge me."

The woman is thin and pale, wearing a peach-colored dress and a straw hat. A cigarette burns between the fingers of her right hand, and a martini glass dangles from her left. It's a Wednesday night in late September, my second year of college, and I'm in a small apartment in Kansas City. I should be 40 miles west, studying in my dorm room. Instead, I journeyed to this party to meet a friend. He promised a wild night of drinking and dancing. Sex was a possibility. With him or with another partygoer. The gathering was a weekly ritual, a Wednesday night meeting for gay men, artists, bohemian poets, defrocked priests, singers and songwriters and other misfits in search of amusement, acceptance, life.

"That's fine," I say to the woman. "I didn't come here to judge."

She eyes me with suspicion. "Good," she says. "There's only one judge in this world, and I just sent him to the bar for another drink."

A wicked grin grows on her face, and I imagine she thinks her comment is amusing, witty, provocative. It strikes me as silly, meaningless, pathetic. I refrain, however, from saying another word. Instead, I smile, wish her well, and walk toward the bar. Another drink sounds good. Another drink will diminish the feelings of insecurity that are growing in my mind. Another drink will make me feel like I belong.

As I near the bar, someone touches my shoulder. I turn to see a handsome man with pale green eyes, a ruddy face. He's much older than me, and his voice offers the dark invitation of seduction when he speaks.

"Enjoying the party?"

"Somewhat." I attempt a smile. "Are you?"

"I will be as soon as we get the hell out of here."

I ask him to repeat the sentence.

"I basically invited you to my place," he says, shaking my hand. "I'm bored. You look bored. I have a full bar and a pool table. Want to?"

Of course I want to. He's handsome. I'm drunk. It's a Wednesday night in late September, my second year of college, and I should be 40 miles west, studying in my dorm room. Instead, I'm drunk.

I'm drunk and I'm following a stranger out the door and into the darkness where he will teach me how to forget myself for a few hours.

———

Find me. I will wait. Capture my heart. I will capture yours. Take this moment to tell me one secret. Breathe this life into your soul. Angels come when we are ready.

Find me.

———

I realize during the early days of my sobriety that the years ahead will be filled with new lessons, not just learning to accept the loss of alcohol as a constant in my life, but also learning to accept myself. I will have to start all over again. I must face pain without self-medication and experience anxiety without erecting a temporary facade built with artificial strength from a bottle.

I know the lessons will be difficult. But I also know that a return to drinking could be a ticket to the final days of my life. For years, I invested in the myth that I could consume alcohol and control its effects without worry or harmful consequences. But after the despair and shame of my final alcoholic hurrah, it is time to admit that I'm powerless over alcohol. It's also time to surrender to self-love and the support offered by friends and family, to accept my weaknesses and insecurities and damage.

It is time to heal, to retrace my steps, understand my motives and mistakes. I will have to learn everything again.

And for the first time in years, I'm ready to try, to move into the future by taking an uncompromising look at my past.

———

"You're cute," the older man says. "Can I see you again?"

It's 6 in the morning, the day after the Wednesday night party, the morning after the night I didn't study for the class that starts in two hours. We're sitting on the sofa in a living room in a house. I have no idea where I am. I don't know this man's name. And I don't want to see him again.

"Yes," I lie. "I'd love to get together sometime."

He reaches over and brushes my cheek with his fingers. "How about tonight?" he whispers. "Dinner? Here? Just you and me?"

"I can't tonight," I lie again. "I have plans."

His eyes flicker for a moment, the rejection registering somewhere behind his pale green gaze.

"That's fine," he says. "Friday night works even better. You can stay the weekend. I have friends coming in from Chicago. They'll like you."

I tell him another lie. I tell him that I have to work Friday night. I tell him I have to work, the weekend is busy, my legs are being amputated, the sky is falling, art does not imitate life, fact is never stranger than fiction, one plus one does not equal two. I tell him so many lies that I become lost in the deception. I kiss him quickly on the lips, pull my T-shirt over my head, walk into the bathroom.

The face in the mirror is strange, foreign. I do not recognize the sad eyes and flat expression and dry lips. I do not know the mask, with its gray shades and thin wrinkles and uneven tones.

"You know what?"

I'm startled. He's followed me into the bathroom, leaning against the door frame, his arms crossed over his chest.

"What?"

"I don't believe you have any intention of seeing me again."

I tell him another lie. I tell him I'd love to see him next week, next month, next year. I tell him up is down, west is east, the sun will not come out tomorrow, the moon is made of cheese, green means stop and red means go. I tell him one lie after the next until he dismisses me with a string of profanity and an invitation to leave his home before he finishes counting to 10.

———

I realize it is time to heal, to retrace my steps, to understand my motives and mistakes. Something is missing from my life, and I'll need to dig deep within my heart, mind, and memories to uncover the truth. With a clear head, the work is possible. With a clean heart, the future is bright. And with a calm spirit, the healing, retracing, understanding will come more readily and with greater purpose than ever before.

I am ready to begin the lessons.

3 / HIGH

I float through the night, disconnected from the earth, detached from the obligations imposed by gravity and sincerity. There is no anchor. No chain or cable or rope restricts my motion. There is no stabilizing force, no firm hold on the surface. I drift through the day, an amber image, pale yellow and translucent in the sun, casting a shadow that shimmers and collapses with the brief mention of contact with reality.

I revel in this blissful state of nothingness. I am happy to savor the high, to fall, to float. Disconnected. Drifting. A vessel lost in a storm, carried by violent currents toward a far point on the edge of the earth, a far point where all lost things disappear.

Where I will disappear.

Forever.

———

Everything spins in a slow-motion curve toward the floor. The walls, a table, bookshelves, a shuttered window. The walls, a print of an Ansel Adams photograph, a woman dressed entirely in black, a ficus tree, another table. *Is it the same table?*

A director's chair collides with my body, wooden arms and tan canvas and metal pieces, as if gravity has been reversed and the objects on the floor are flying upward. The chair collapses with an angry snap, something breaks somewhere, creating a sound like the crack of a limb when it's ripped from a tree.

There's pain. My cheek, my wrist, my legs. I look over and see an electrical outlet, the baseboard, a child's toy. I think: *I'm falling.* But it's already over. I'm down, flat on the floor. I feel like laughing, yelling, screaming. I'm confused and there is blood on my face and I hear a baby crying and a man telling someone that I'm a good friend.

He says, "We can't just ask him to leave, Susan. He's hurt."

I must be at Steve and Susan's house. Steve is a former coworker. Susan is his wife, a woman who disapproves of my friendship with Steve because I bring chaos and anxiety into their home. She is generally polite and patient, but tonight is different. Tonight she is firm and relentless in her desire for me to leave.

From a place far away, I hear Susan. "He's not hurt, Steve. He's drunk. Now get him out of here."

Cold air on my face. I can feel cold air and hear the tires hissing on the wet pavement. Street lights flare and fade, flooding the car's interior with hard white light before they vanish. There's cold air and I feel so high, so fucking high. Wish I were home. Wish I had a beer. Thinking: *Maybe I have a beer at home. I could go out and buy a bottle of Vitamin V. Do I have cigarettes? Is it Saturday?*

We stop. A sudden jerk and the car stops moving and I'm walking, someone is holding my arm and I'm walking up the sidewalk to my apartment building. Cold air fills my lungs, big frozen pillows of air. Thinking: *Where's my coat? Did I have a jacket? No, shit. It's Sunday. Where can I buy Vitamin V? What time is it?*

I'm inside. Steve is talking. He's standing in the open door, one foot in the hallway, quivering with the need to not be here, to be finished with this messy night.

"You gonna be OK?"

I say something. He says something. He's gone.

I'm alone and it's 10 o'clock and I'm out of cigarettes and I'm going out the back to buy Vitamin V. Thinking: *If I pace this right, I can keep the high going, keep flying, feel even better than I do now. I can go forever. I don't have to tell anyone anything anymore. It's just me. And I'm gone.*

———

OK, I admit it. I miss being high. I miss it, but I've found a replacement for the buzz, the click, the whirl of soaring. In certain circles, that admission would be considered traitorous. *Did he say what I think he said? Is he serious? How can he miss something that nearly killed him? Why would he?*

Why? I'm human. And I'm honest. And there are some aspects of drinking I miss.

Such as?

I miss the hit, the swoosh of being light-headed, the sensation of liquidity, the rush of intoxication, the release of tension. In the beginning, I miss it every day of every week. It's like the first few days that follow the end of a romance, the period when you fear you'll never again feel whole or complete, because the void that remains when your lover is gone from your life aches and trembles and fills you with loneliness. I concentrate on the memories, trying to keep them alive, struggling to separate them from the nuclear explosion that coincided with Dylan's departure. I focus on the sense of flying after the first three or four drinks, when the reason I wanted to drink was momentarily extinguished; the fear deflated, the anxiety quieted, the self-hatred seduced, the void filled.

———

Hush. Don't make a sound. Not one soft sound. If I stay just like this forever, nothing will happen to my high. I can fold myself into an accordion, hug my knees to my chest, find the warmth that's been missing. Stay like this forever.

Nothing like this feeling. Nothing to duplicate the freedom and slow stroll down into a secret place where I can watch the world and it cannot hurt me. I cannot be bruised here in this secret place. Nothing like this feeling, this freedom.

Yes, I'll have another one. Thank you. Vitamin V rocks with a twist, please. Vitamin V rocks with a twist of the key that unlocks the next plateau and takes me higher. One more step up, one more step away from the murmur and decay of this life.

Hush. Don't make a sound. Not one soft sound. If I stay just like this forever, nothing will happen to my high.

———

"What's wrong with just one glass of wine?"

Chet stands in the middle of his kitchen, removing the cork from a bottle of pinot grigio. I'm having coffee with cream. He started the afternoon with kiwi-strawberry juice over ice and decided to switch to wine as soon as dusk darkened to night.

"One glass is not going to kill you," Chet says sarcastically. "It's not like you'll get high or anything."

"That's just the point," I say, stepping in to defend my sobriety once again. "It's the 'anything' that scares me. I tried to have just one glass of wine a few years ago, and that ended up ruining my relationship with Dylan and nearly costing me my life."

Chet fills his glass, squeaks the cork back into the bottle, leans against the granite countertop and blazes me with a smug smile. "Why are you so dramatic about this shit?"

As Chet swirls the wine in his glass and dips his nose in for a fragrance check, I wonder why I agreed to join him for the day. Is it to test my fortitude? Whenever Chet and I get together these days, he inevitably begins to chip away at my choice to quit drinking.

"I mean, what the hell," Chet says, breaking the silence. "Don't you miss it?"

"Sure I miss it. I wish I could feel some of the effects without drinking. I wish I could have that woozy, happy, carefree sense of numbness."

Chet smiles and holds his glass out. "You can," he says. "Just have one glass. It won't hurt."

"Thanks, Chet. I'm OK without it. I've found alternative ways to feel high."

He blasts a laugh. "Like what? Dope?"

I shake my head. "No," I tell him. "Just living a clean life gets me high. Being able to make decisions based on rational thought and not my fucked up hormones or anxieties. That's the biggest charge in the world for me now. That's what gets me off."

I watch his reaction. He's like most people; a faint grin, a barely detectable nod of the head. He doesn't believe me. He doesn't think it's possible for an alcoholic to live without liquor. As if a single, sober life is impossible.

———

The guy behind the counter is talking. I can't find my money. I slow down and start over. Check my front pockets first and then the back pockets. No money.

"I'm sorry," I say. "I left my cash in the truck. Be right back."

Fuck, it's getting colder. Open the ashtray, pull a fresh twenty from inside, listen to the collection of lucky pennies rattle when I close the tray. It's an odd place to keep money, but it works for me. Slam the door. Thinking: *Hurry. This is taking too long. It's fucking cold and this is taking too long and why is that guy staring at me?*

"You're bleeding." He points at his left cheek, right below his eye. "Do you want a paper towel or something?"

"Oh, shit." I touch my cheek. It's wet and my fingers stick to the partially dried blood. "Thanks for telling me."

Outside, walking to the truck, taking a deep breath of the frozen air. Thinking: *Jesus. I'm such an asshole. I'm getting sloppy. Everyone's going to know. That's OK. Fuck them. I don't need anybody. I don't need anybody. I don't need anybody.*

Home now. Sad. Lights down low, a ribbon of smoke rises from a stick of Spiritual Guide burning in the kitchen sink, incense to sweeten the flat, stale air. A glass from the cabinet. No ice. Just warm Vitamin V from the bottle. Cigarette. Thinking: *Susan and Steve are never going to invite me over for dinner again. I probably scared the kids. I broke something. Did I break something? Fuck them. It's not the end of the world. Who needs them? Was it a chair? Yes. I broke a chair. That's why I'm bleeding. I can't believe the liquor store guy saw it. I must've looked like a fucking skid row fucking bum.*

More Vitamin V. A fresh cigarette. Walk out back and look at the stars burning in the icy sky, looking for a constellation of hope and rescue and seeing nothing but flat black arcing overhead with the tiny points of hot white light.

Back inside. Warmer. Lock the door. No company. Close the blinds. I'll just call in sick tomorrow so I can sleep and forget this day, forget the broken chair and the blood and the nothingness that wraps around me now like a misplaced friend. Welcome, night. Flying high in the darkness. I can hear my head clicking, feel my veins expand and contract—life leaving through a bruised entrance—the stillness of sleep staying just outside of my reach. Waiting for dawn. Waiting for something. Waiting. And still high when the morning arrives with the promise of a new day. I wish I remembered what that signified for me. I think I knew at one point, but now I only know that I'm spinning in a slow-motion curve. The walls, a table, bookshelves, a shuttered window. The walls, a print of an Ansel Adams photograph, a woman dressed entirely in black.

I know her name, but I will not speak it.

Good night, death.

Hello, sweet, precious high.

4 / Empty Sorrow

It's 2 in the morning, time for the sidewalk sale outside the bar at the end of the night. The usual suspects wobble around, smoking and staring, whispers and invitations. The Vitamin V vampires appear, lean forms that materialize from the shadows and crowd the view like hungry tourists peering into cages at the zoo.

They want his flesh and spit and fire. Want him to surrender, abandon values and virtues and come home for the night. They want him to become a moaning shape rolling in the dark, legs locked together, arms linked tightly. They want sweat to form on his forehead as he straddles their waists, sipping a beer that waits on the bedside table. Want him to drag his nails down their back, a swerving red two-lane road that leads to the inevitable payoff.

They want him. Want everything. Want it now.

And he goes. Again and again. Another night, the scent of freshly laundered sheets, unfamiliar floor plans, someone else's coffee cup in the morning, a new bar of soap and clean towels and the fair exchange of one phone number for another.

"Thanks," they say the next morning. "I had a great time."

"Yeah." He's had this hollow conversation a million times. "Call me."

They take his flesh, his moments of clarity, and they leave him with regrets and split images and the fractured memories that follow the endless nights of senseless drinking. Blackouts and white lies, the dark crevices that draw him down and surround him with something that he wants and nothing that he needs.

Drinking is death. *Hey, what's your name?* He wants a drink. *I think we go to the same gym.* He buys one more Vitamin V rocks. *Want to dance?* Swallows it fast and keeps moving. *Can I call you?* Takes a minute to think, to breathe, to regain balance. *Aren't you dating someone?* There's the door and the humid night. *Let's get together sometime.* One more Vitamin V rocks. *Can I have a cigarette?* And then he's out in the night for the sidewalk sale and everyone standing in the streetlight's bleached, stale shimmer. *What are you doing now?* Keys in his back pocket, tucked behind a stack of flat bills. *Want to come over?* He's standing in the hard light talking to a couple with sweet smiles and Lucifer's game book and an address in Westwood. *C'mon over for a while. We'll have fun.*

He knows he should go home, go to bed, but it's 2 in the morning and he doesn't want to go home, to bed, alone. It's 2 in the morning and he knows what he wants, knows who he wants.

It's 2 in the morning and he loses again.

————

"What happened to you last night?"

Whenever this question is posed, I never know quite how

to answer. What happened? Nothing. Everything. Something in between. Crucible incidents. Events of no importance. Staying in. Going out. Another escape into the smoke filled shadows at The Edge, gripping my glass and watching the crowd for someone appealing. Hours of intrigue and innuendo followed by sweat and lust and the arc of life spilling from inside, leaving semen-stained sheets in a house on Summit Street. A loft in the River Market. An apartment overlooking The Country Club Plaza.

Leaving intuition and common sense and responsibility at the curb. Disregarding fate. Taking no notice of future feelings or past mistakes.

"What happened to you last night?"

"I met someone."

They snicker. "Someone?"

"Don't push it," I say. "Just leave it alone."

"Spill it," they say. "Tell me everything."

I refuse, deflecting their demand with a joke or an abrupt conversational swerve.

"Are you going to David's on Saturday?"

They laugh. "He must've been pretty hot if you won't talk about it."

So I talk. I describe his good qualities and delete the obvious red flags. I talk about his dog or his musical preferences or the other thin threads of mutuality that connected us for one night. I include every detail with one exception. I fail to report my inebriated state. But that goes without saying. Anyone who knows me is aware of my fondness for alcohol. Anyone who knows me has witnessed my self-destructive dance. Anyone who knows me collects the clues that scatter into the air whenever I recount my exploits.

And then, my monologue complete, I take a breath and they ask a question I hadn't considered, a question I don't anticipate, a question that amuses me and scares me when I realize I don't have an answer.

"What's his name?"

His name? I don't remember. I have a vague idea of where he lives, the street and neighborhood, the color of the walls in his bedroom. But his name?

———

In the drinking days, details like names and addresses and the consequences of unsafe sex are as meaningless as the contents of an aspirin tablet or a Prozac capsule or a well-tempered moment in time. Who needs names when you remain invisible and untouched by life's prosperity and true pleasures? Names are worthless when you seek a numb place far from home. Names are not the currency you value. Names are obstacles, useless information, troublesome particulars that will do nothing more than remind you of the previous night's empty sorrow.

———

Find me. I will wait. Capture my heart. I will capture yours. Take this moment to tell me one secret. Breathe this life into your soul. Angels come when we are ready.

Find me.

———

I write lists constantly to convince myself that things are running smoothly and I'm maintaining contact with life. Daily lists and weekly lists. Projects I plan to write and items I need to buy. Deodorant and a novel about the Virgin Mary and toilet paper. Send a card to Joan in Boston. Milk and coffee. Exchange the Jimmy Somerville CD for Nusrat Fateh Ali Khan. Call Mom so she doesn't worry about me. Laundry detergent and cat food.

The lists sit on top of the cabinet in the living room. I date them to add emphasis and urgency to their role in my life. When deadlines arrive and depart without action, I change the date or rewrite the lists to remove the sense of failure I feel when I cannot find the time to buy laundry detergent but have been very successful in purchasing and consuming two fifths of Absolut in the past six days.

Failure. We were surprised by his inability to accomplish simple tasks.

Failure. His attempt to follow fundamental nutritional guidelines seemed to be a labor in vain.

Failure. The patient's efforts to stay sober proved unsuccessful.

———

"I've got vodka," the voice says. "A fresh bottle in the freezer. Want to play?"

It's a Sunday in May, a year before I quit, a year before I burn my bridge to Liquor Land.

I wish I hadn't answered the phone, but it's too late. I think: *Who is this? I don't recognize the voice. Where do these men come from and why won't they go away?*

He repeats his question.

"Play what?" I say. "I'm not sure I know how."

"You did last week." There's a brief pause for what I imagine he intends to be dramatic effect, and the voice adds, "Or at least that's what I heard from Don."

"Dan?"

"Don," the voice says again. He adds a last name and waits for the information to register. Considering it's barely 1 o'clock and I was out until 8, the connection takes a lot longer than it would on a good day.

"Oh," I say finally. "The guy from Houston?"

"No," the voice says. "From right here in Kansas City."

It is easy to negotiate these calls when they come. Telephone tricks. Doorbell trade. The hit-and-run lust of a network of men who feign interest until they're stretched out in their beds with a satisfied smile on their face and a swirl of viscid, white fluid on their stomach, running down their back, dotting their chest. And then, after they've mouthed silent sentiments and soaked the air with their animal frenzy, when you're standing in the bathroom trying to recognize your face in the mirror, they thank you for coming over and ask you to come back again. Soon. Sometime. Later in the week. But you don't return because you lose the phone number or forget the address. You misplace the combination to this mixture of Vitamin V and sex. You distance yourself from the act because your high is fading and you wonder why you agreed to meet this stranger for an intimate exchange.

"So you have time to stop by?" the voice asks. "I'll be around all evening."

"Sure. Why not? Dan's a good guy. I trust his instincts."

"Don." The voice corrects my error. "His name's Don. What time will you be here?"

"Twenty minutes?"

The voice gives an address near the Nelson-Atkins Museum, a house on Rockhill Road, a bungalow with waxed oak plank floors and green velvet drapes and a fresh bottle of Vitamin V. Two glasses, the seal breaks on the bottle, the magic sound of misery poured over ice.

His name is Eric. A handsome man, mid 30s, blue contact lenses and gray-tinged stubble on his chin. A pair of faded Levi's, an AIX T-shirt, Mickey Mouse wristwatch. We sit in the living room to begin the evening. Eric tells me that he and Don were once lovers and are now friends. They travel together, own a business together, spend holidays together.

"Sounds like you're still a couple." I lick the rim of the glass, tasting the Vitamin V, anticipating the rush. "Where is he tonight?"

Eric looks at the framed photographs on the mantel. I recognize the man who shares the frame with Eric, someone I met at a party a few weeks earlier. This must be Don, but I can't make the connection between the face in the picture and the name. I remember the way he kissed, the sound he made when I bit his nipples, the apartment where we spent the night.

"I have a confession to make," Eric tells me. "Don and I are still together. We have an open relationship."

I laugh. "Very open," I say. "But that works for me. Don't worry. We'll have fun."

Eric smiles. "I know we will," he says. "Don told me all about you."

So that's who I've become. A commodity shared by lovers. An object meant to be discussed and evaluated. A source of sexual amusement for anyone with an unopened bottle of Vitamin V and freshly laundered sheets, unfamiliar floor plans, someone else's coffee cup in the morning, a new bar of soap, clean towels, and the fair exchange of one phone number for another.

"Thanks. I had a great time."

"Yeah. Call me."

5 / Shallow Mercy

We tell ourselves stories. We tell ourselves lies and fabrications. And at some point during the drunken days and soulless nights, after reciting the lies and stories with the artful nuances and patience of a Socratic academician, the lies become truth. Truth becomes foreign. And we are lost.

We create our stories from fragments of memory, shards of sentiment, images observed through eyes weakened by fatigue and intolerance.

We watch the horizon for signs of trouble. Unexpected visitors. Notes of reproach that follow unattractive and public displays of drunkenness. The uneasy silence that envelops a group of friends when we arrive for dinner, late and mumbling and scented with Vitamin V and cigarettes. Concerned inquiries that arc through the air and spark an immediate desire to disappear.

Signs of trouble.
Stories and lies.
Memory and sentiment.

———

I started drinking when I was a child. I stopped six months before I turned 40. At the age of 26, I began a nine-year "honeymood" as a dry drunk. I call it a honeymood because a relatively peaceful surface concealed a core of turmoil and turbulence. Dry drunks may abstain from alcohol, but they don't seek solutions to the problems that contribute to their alcoholism. They don't heal.

During my decades of drinking, I exchanged normalcy for imbalance and self-respect for dread. Alcohol made it less difficult to meet new people and easy to disregard old friends. Drinking made it possible to ignore the obvious and obsess about the trivial. I ignored the consequences of turning away from the people who were important in my life. I turned my back on sober living with zeal and dedication, convinced I could navigate the river of alcohol unscathed and unblemished. Drinking may be a problem for some men, but it was part of my daily ritual. I could handle it. I could continue the demonic waltz, flirting with danger and avoiding tragedy. I was invincible. I was unmarked. I could juggle the balls, maintain the fiction, dance on the razor's edge without harm.

I was wrong.

———

There are many reasons we drink: we're lonely, sad, tired. We drink to celebrate events and commemorate achievements. We drink when our personal lives fail to meet our expectations. We drink because David left us for Tony who left Brian for David. We drink because we want to shed the inhibitions that keep us at home on Friday night instead of out at a club. We drink because the clubs have grown tiresome.

We drink because we're too fat, too tall, too shy. We drink because everyone else drinks. Because we want to mourn the loss of a favored job or mark the accomplishment of a new assignment. We drink because we're angry, impatient, anxious.

Some of us drink because we are ashamed of our sexuality. Whether on the surface or subliminally, we are hounded by the negative images and messages about same-sex orientation that we confront on a daily basis. We are made ashamed by our families, our coworkers, our friends, by the things they say and the things they do to remind us that we are somehow less valued, less important, less meaningful because we love men.

———

The center does not hold when you're an alcoholic because there is no center. Nor is there a clear moment when the rules of discipline and respect are no longer involved, when the act of erosion is complete. We're operating with an incomplete set of tools, a partial set of guidelines, an interchangeable collection of excuses and reasons and attitudes.

The invitations arrive, we accept politely, knowing the chances are slim that we'll actually attend the event. We miss the birthday party because we had an unexpected visitor from New York. The unexpected visitor from New York arrived on a plane that was delayed by a storm in Chicago. We failed to meet the unexpected visitor's plane because there was a flat tire and an unresponsive tow truck driver and a cell phone that carried a battery that had been bled of its life by the many calls to explain why we weren't going to be at the birthday party.

Dinner with a group of friends sounds appealing at noon,

but eight hours later the slow and deliberate toll of a series of Vitamin V and tonic concoctions renders us unable to attend. The solution is simple and without courage: When we're certain the group of friends has already departed the apartment where everyone agreed to meet before heading to the restaurant, we dial the seven digits and leave a message of apology and regret.

In the times I'm writing about, messages of apology and regret were common dispatches. The pattern was inexplicable. There was no unexpected visitor from New York. I'd borrowed a car from a drinking acquaintance to drive to a liquor store, where I'd surrendered $20 for a bottle of Absolut and a pack of Marlboros, where I sat and used the car phone to call and say that I would be unable to attend the birthday party.

Like many of the events of those days, the birthday party was the only tangible detail, the only thing that was real. Everything else was fabrication and deceit and fear. Like many of the events of those days, everything else was a lie.

I agree to meet Finn and Melissa at the Classic Cup for Sunday brunch. On Sunday, instead of arriving at the restaurant at the appointed hour, I awake in a house in Armour Hills, tangled between Graham and Ross with the leaden weight of a hangover pressing on my head. Graham is a marketing executive whose Brooks Brothers shirts mask angular black tattoo bands that encircle his biceps. Ross is Graham's lover, a former member of the LAPD who replaced his badge and department-issue revolver with a gold hoop earring and a devastating smile.

"Can I use the phone?"

The tattooed love boy smiles. "Sure. It's in the library."

I dial Finn's house and leave a message, a brief monologue laced with inaccurate statements and deflated apologies. I hang up the phone, walk into the kitchen, find the Vitamin V bottle from the night before. A quick swig, a swallow of orange juice and I return to the bedroom.

"You OK?" Ross asks. "You don't look so good."

"Everything's fine," I say. "Everything's just great."

———

Nothing is fine. Nothing works. Nothing holds together. When you're actively drinking, there is no continuity between thought and action, between day and night. You believe that all is well and life is defined by coherence and order. But the chaos that hums just beneath the surface undermines every shallow mercy that you can find in your waking hours.

You lose focus. You misplace momentum. You become a hollow and silent shadow. Secrets begin to collect as you explain why you missed work yesterday, why the promise was broken, why the knock at your door went unanswered.

You hide. You transfer facts from one fictitious excuse to the next. You remain static and unmoving, mute and blind to the cracks that are revealed in your character, the causal elements that seduce you into the next cocktail, another night at the bar, the unwanted advances of a stranger.

The evidence is everywhere, but your eyes are trained to identify only those elements of the puzzle that do not cause pain. You find reasons for the symptoms. You missed work because the fatigue was unbearable. You broke the promise because it should never have been made in the first place. And you ignored the knock at the door because you knew who you'd find on the other side.

Friends become expendable. Family becomes irrelevant. Everything you once cherished becomes random and morose. Liquor makes it seem less important. Less weighty.

Less burdensome. And, in the end, less meaningful.

Life becomes death. Death becomes a dream. Dreams become nightmares. And nightmares became reality.

———

I meet Graham and Ross on a Saturday night at the Dixie Belle, one of Kansas City's more popular gay clubs. Situated in a fatigued neighborhood between the downtown business district and Crown Center's collection of glass-ribbed walkways, granite-faced office buildings, and sun-showered courtyards, the Dixie Belle is surrounded by warehouses and industrial workshops and art galleries opened by urban pioneers.

In the drinking days, I went to the DB for two reasons: to drink and to trick. On some nights, I achieved both goals. On other occasions, I returned home alone, inebriated and frustrated.

The night I meet Graham and Ross, I'm talking to Eric about his boyfriend's new job in Atlanta. Eric doesn't want to lose the boyfriend, but he doesn't want to move. I listen to the story and advise Eric to follow his heart.

"I don't have a heart," he tells me. "And I'm tired of pretending that I do."

We stand and watch the crowd. Men in wide-brimmed black cowboy hats and chaps and leather armbands. A drag queen with a mountainous swirl of blonde hair and a bad scar on her cheek. An obese man in a tangerine-colored shirt, sitting on the pool table with a thin guy wearing a dog collar.

After a few minutes, I excuse myself and wander out to the patio. The awnings have been removed and you can see the stars above. I buy a fresh drink, turn around and see Graham standing nearby. He smiles and raises his drink. He looks friendly and approachable, the kind of man I'd like to investigate with my hands and my mouth and my tongue.

"What's up?" he says when I walk over. "Looks like you're having a good time."

"Yep. So far, so good."

We stand and talk about working out and the heat and a trip he's planning to Palm Springs. As he describes his last visit to California, Ross walks up and drops his arm over Graham's shoulders.

"You guys ready to go?" Ross winks at me. "I've had enough of this freak show."

Graham introduces me to Ross and says, "Want to come over for a swim?"

I hadn't planned on a threesome, but they're handsome, pleasant, friendly. And I'm drunk. The chemistry is correct, the equation is balanced. It's another night for lust and lost intentions and whatever may happen next.

———

"Vodka OK with you?" Graham hands me a large cobalt-blue tumbler. "I thought we could all use a little night-cap."

We drink and listen to John Coltrane. Sorrowful saxophone, candles flickering on the mantel, a wall of bookcases filled with leather-bound books, monstrous ceramic pieces, framed photographs of Graham and Ross and their friends. It's a seductive setting, the kind of first-date ambience that often follows dinner and a movie. The illusions of romance and temptation are wasted on us. We're not here for romance.

One or two drinks later and we're in the pool, the night sky punctuated with a spray of white diamonds, the same stars I saw earlier at the DB. Graham swims up behind me, runs his hands down my back, whispers in my ear.

"Need another drink?"

I shake my head. "In a few minutes." I reach for the box of cigarettes on the slate terrace. "I'm OK for now."

Graham eliminates the space between us, wraps his arms around my shoulders, rubs my nipples with his thumbs, warms the back of my neck with his moist breath. As I turn my head to accept his kiss, Ross swims toward us. He licks my neck and joins the kiss, our three tongues wrestling with urgency and heat.

"You like this feeling?" a voice says in my ear. "You like this taste?"

Another voice, another question. Wet, sloppy kisses. Hands on my waist, my shoulders, between my legs.

"You like the way I touch you?"

Another moment, another kiss.

"You want more?" a voice murmurs behind my head. "The boy want more of this good thing?"

The Vitamin V has replaced the blood in my veins and eliminated reason and choice. I am liquid, a willing participant in the fluidity and force of the carnal dance that binds man to man. Tongues. Lips. Fingers. Hands. Hard flesh on hard flesh. The languid water lapping at our shoulders and torsos and faces. An aromatic curtain descending from the pots of flowers on the terrace. A large white candle flickering on the poolside table.

I know I should be home in bed. But I don't care about work, about tomorrow, about responsibility and duty and the correctness of adult obligations. I want these men, these lustful creatures, these constructs of power and grace. I want more Vitamin V. Another cigarette. A dozen more nights exactly like this one. I want to drown in the night, the shadows, the loose comfort of blind hedonism. The slippery fire of another weighty kiss. More Vitamin V. Another cigarette. More sex.

I know I should leave now. But I don't care. And I don't think. Instead, I do what I've done so many times before. I do what has perpetuated this agony and allowed the demons to wrap their bloodstained fingers ever more tightly around my soul. I do what comes so naturally now that I'm losing myself, drowning, falling further into the hole.

I surrender.

6 / SORRY

I'm falling apart, sinking, losing my grip. Reality separates into small fragments, compartments of activity that make the attempts to disentangle my drinking life from my regular life pointless. The days are structured, finite parcels of time and energy that will allow me to reach my goal: drinking.

Does anyone know what's happening? Can anyone see? Do they know I'm dying?

I start to think I can manage this system of deception and paper-thin honor. I find scribbled notes in my pockets, names and phone numbers and clues to my whereabouts the night before. I want answers but avoid the questions. I wish I knew why I feel displaced, a constant stranger, an unwanted visitor. I wish Dylan could surrender his fear and truly embrace our relationship. I wish I could be honest with him about my drinking.

Does anyone know what's happening?

The days blur and blend, a week passes and then a month and I'm in the same place: Nowhere. I go through the motions, work and paying the bills and dinner out with friends. A trip to Phoenix. A drive in the country. A fund-raiser at The Unicorn Theater.

And always I drink. Secretly, before anyone comes to my apartment, while they're running errands. I hide the bottles beneath the kitchen sink, tucked in the corner behind the cat food and laundry detergent and trash bags. I wrap the bottles inside newspapers, seal the newspapers in a plastic bag, carry the plastic bag out to the curb.

Does anyone know?

———

I go to work, to the gym, to dinner with friends. I return phone calls only when absolutely necessary, sometimes days later, sometimes the following month. I struggle to conform to the standards of common courtesy and the rules of social propriety. Yes, thank you. No, I don't care for any. Could I please have another refill on my Prozac and a couple of those Stoli bottles wrapped to go?

Excuses come as easily and as often as the rising sun. Dylan discovers an empty half-pint tucked beneath the seat in my truck. I tell him it's ancient history, nothing to worry about, a forgotten relic. I'm sorry. It will never happen again. Reed learns that I lied about the reason I skipped his party. I admit that it's true; I was drunk and disorderly at Lana's house in Louisburg. Reed screams and yells and says he'll never talk to me again. I'm sorry. It will never happen again. Julian arrives early to pick me up for dinner, peers through the kitchen window, sees me drinking from a bottle of chardonnay. He's fierce in his disappointment, telling me that I violated our pact to remain sober.

I'm sorry.

It will never happen again.

But it does.

And why not? If I don't care about the consequences, why should anyone else be interested? I'm an adult. I know what I'm doing. I'm in control. Things are fine. It's OK. Everything will work out. Everything will be great. Things will get better. I'll stop drinking. I promise. I'll go to AA meetings. I'll go to therapy sessions. Whatever it takes. I promise.

Lying is easier than breathing. Lying is everything.

———

I drink willingly and often, rarely sipping a cocktail unless I am in the company of others. I drink with a thirst that has nothing to do with a biological need for liquid. I drink during the day, small shots of Vitamin V between cups of coffee. I drink at night, quick bursts of alcohol after my daily workout, before my boyfriend arrives for dinner.

Drinking is no longer about pleasure. It's become a necessity, a self-inflicted torture, cocktail suicide, liquid lobotomy. Drinking and sex become my barometer, the way I measure my place in the world. The imbalanced logic and unhealthy consequences become easy to accept if I swallow enough Vitamin V. In the deep recesses of my mind, I know I'm sick, that I'm losing the fight, but I can't turn back. The lightening sharp pleasure of the rush of alcohol through my body is more important that life itself. The searing heat of the first drink on an empty stomach is my holy communion.

I'm falling apart.

I'm going down.

I'm sinking.

Does anyone know what's happening?

Does anyone care?

7 / Vacant Moments

The days are bland and static, identical periods of inter-changeable dread. I fear the prospect of discovery and cloak my actions, my breath, my heart in numbing layers of explanation, mouthwash, insensate experiences of repetitive lust.

I try to remember when drinking became the focus of my life. When it evolved from a social activity to an act that defined every day of every month. When it grew into an obsession that influenced my every move.

I worry that I drink too much. I worry that I drink too often. I worry that I worry too much about drinking. Through it all, I worry. And through it all, I drink.

———

"How's it going?"

I look up. Inquisitive blue eyes. A blond crew cut. Teeth like polished pearls framed by a tanned, muscular smile. He tilts his head to one side and repeats the question. It's another Saturday night at the Cabaret, another opportunity to fuel my demons with Vitamin V and find a man who will tell me I'm handsome and sexy and desirable.

The Cabaret is on Main Street in Kansas City, surrounded by a supermarket, a Swiss tea shop and bakery, hair salons, a dry cleaner, and a preschool. The exterior's putty-colored stucco walls and darkened windows are far from inviting. Inside, the space is dingy and soiled. Three bars, a tiny dance floor, pool tables, and pinball machines. On weekend nights, The Cabaret is a crowded swamp of attitude and feeble fashion clones and slaves to the rhythm.

"Buy you a drink?" the blond crew cut asks.

I smile. "Sure," I say. "That'd be great."

As I watch, he turns to the bartender and orders a pair of Cape Cods, two Vitamin V-and-cranberry tickets to a night of seductive flirtation and delicious possibilities. His name is Grant, he lives in Toronto, he's visiting Kansas City for a week. Business meetings punctuated with workouts at Gold's Gym and casual sex with Midwestern men.

"Cheers," Grant says, passing me a tumbler filled with the soft red elixir that has become my favorite cocktail in the past few weeks. "What's your name?"

I introduce myself, shake his hand, lean in to hear his next question.

"You from here?"

"More or less," I say, giving my standard reply to the standard query. "I'm a product of the Midwest. Conceived in Chicago, born in Des Moines, raised in Kansas City."

He takes the information with a wide grin. "I like your look," he tells me. "Want to dance?"

Alcoholism is like a shifting plane of sand, a shadow without a source, a storm system that sweeps through you with a deadly and seductive force. In textbooks and medical journals and intellectual discourse, the disease is defined and debated.

For alcoholics, these discussions are meaningless. When the next drink is your only thought, the last thing you want is someone asking if you're familiar with the nine characteristics of the alcoholic as presented by the American Psychiatric Association. When your mind spins with an intricate puzzle of pain and an uncertain future, you're not likely to prowl the stacks at a nearby library in search of a revised edition of the *Diagnostic and Statistical Manual of Mental Disorders,* where you'll find the nine characteristics explained in crisp, lifeless language and a black-and-white sincerity.

In the drinking days, I wanted oceans of Vitamin V and easy access to mindless sex, not a voice saying, "One of the characteristics is: alcohol often taken in larger amounts or over a longer period than the person intended."

Did I care that another red flag was "persistent desire or one or more unsuccessful efforts to cut down or control alcohol use"?

When it was 2 o'clock on a Sunday afternoon and I was still in bed, a position necessitated by a pounding headache and ceaseless nausea, I didn't want someone to suggest that I might be an alcoholic if I invested a "great deal of time…in activities necessary to get alcohol, taking the substance, or recovering from its effects."

And the other representative or symbolic traits? I knew them well. I was familiar with the act of avoiding "social, occupational, or recreational activities" due to frequent intoxication and withdrawal symptoms. No one needed to tell me about "continued alcohol use despite knowledge of having a persistent or recurrent social, psychological, or physical problem that is caused or exacerbated by the use of the substance." I'd had my chipped teeth repaired and my sprained ankle taped and the deep puncture wound in my arm bandaged.

Physical wounds heal. Some leave scars, others leave ghost imprints on your memory. But the spiritual damage caused by alcoholism is something that may never heal. Choices are made, options are exercised, and the drinker is left with little more than blurred recollections and tangled illusions of a time when hope was a viable alternative and dreams held a faint pulse of life.

———

Grant stands in my living room, slowly unbuttoning his Levi's. I stand in my bedroom doorway, following his movements, removing my khakis as he steps out of his 501s. He pulls his T-shirt over his head, unveiling a massive chest and a Maple Leaf tattoo on his left shoulder.

"Come here," he says. "Let's see what you taste like."

I walk into the living room, grab my drink, swallow the last half inch of Vitamin V.

"I taste like Stoli," I say. "How about you?"

He unzips my pullover with his teeth. When the shirt falls open, Grant slips his hands inside and eases it over my shoulders. We melt together and I can smell his cologne, the same scent I wear. I can also smell the residue of cigarette smoke from the bar, the hint of beer on his breath.

"Let's have one more drink," he says after a long kiss. "I could use just a bit more edge."

While he fixes the Vitamin V rocks, I search for an old Nina Simone CD.

"Here you go." Grant hands me a glass. "Cheers."

"Cheers." I gulp the Stoli and wipe my lips.

When Grant finishes his Vitamin V, he starts kneading my shoulders with his hands.

"Want a back rub?"

"Sure."

We go into the bedroom and I light a pair of votive candles. I climb into bed and flop onto my stomach; Grant climbs on top of me and begins to rub my shoulders and back. I can feel the Vitamin V burning in my throat, kicking in, blending with the drinks I had earlier at the Cabaret. I relax into the massage, the feel of his hands, the sound of his voice as he describes what he plans to do to me in a few minutes. I'm beginning to doze, and I try to fight the feeling. I can hear the music in the living room, the soothing melody, the sound of Grant's voice, the tension leaving my muscles, the Vitamin V lulling me into a warm, quiet place.

When I wake a few hours later, the sun is up and Grant is gone. I roll over and try to get my bearings. My head pounds with a fierce hangover and my throat tastes like dirt. I look at the clock. It's a few minutes after 1. I look around the room, trying to remember what happened, straining to pull the clues together into a complete whole.

I walk into the living room. No Grant. The door is unlocked, the stereo is off. A pair of aspirin and a glass of water. I check the phone messages, look for a note. Nothing. I remember driving home, the Stoli after we reached my apartment, the massage in bed.

I go into the bathroom, open the medicine cabinet, pull out the toothpaste.

And that's when it hits me. My cologne is gone. Both bottles. $100. Terrific, I think. Grant's a thief. I go into the kitchen to see if my money is gone. And it is. Another $50. Luckily, he didn't take my credit cards, my watch, the keys to my car.

———

"Oh, Jesus. He could've killed you!" Ann screams. "What were you thinking?"

I called Ann to report the incident, not to receive a maternal admonition. I deserve her severe reproof, her words of warning. I was lucky and I know it. I trusted Grant, if that was actually his name, because I was drunk and he came on to me at the bar. I was drowning in Vitamin V and itching to connect for sex. One plus one equals two. Boy meets boy. Boy eats boy. Boy is left alone. Over the years, I'd become so adept at the elementary logic and lustful mathematics, I never thought about danger or consequences. I went into homes and apartments and hotel rooms with strangers. I came out alive. Some men aren't so lucky. Until Grant, I never realized the extent of my good fortune.

"Did you learn your lesson?" Ann asks. "No more unknowns. OK?"

"OK."

"No more one-night stands."

I hesitate. How can I make this pledge? Without my steady diet of empty sex and Vitamin V, I will not exist. The brief encounters and lost weekends and vacant moments are the only things I want to collect. Going to work and spending time with friends and maintaining the exterior appearances of normalcy are a fair exchange for entry to my secret, dark world.

"Well?" Ann isn't going to let this rest. "Promise?"

"I'll try."

"That's not good enough. I don't want to get a call some day telling me you've been murdered by a freak in the middle of the night. Your life is worth more than sex with some guy."

"OK," I lie. "I'll be careful."

"Promise me."

"What?"

"Promise me that you won't do this again. Why don't you find someone? Get into a relationship? You can do it."

I think about Andrew in Denver and Finn in Kansas City and David in New York. Three strikes and I'm out.

"I promise," I tell Ann. "No more."

I hang up and hope she believes me, hope somebody believes me, because I can't believe myself.

8 / FUEL

The back seat of a black sedan at midnight on a Thursday, Flynn at the wheel, slamming down Mercier Street with incredible disregard for the cars parked at the curb, the people sleeping in the bungalows and apartment buildings, the safety of the passengers in the backseat of the black sedan.

It's midnight on a Thursday, another opportunity to ingest as much fuel as possible and ignite a scorched-earth agenda through this night into tomorrow morning, when I'll scramble into the shower at 7 o'clock and scrub the scales of dried semen from my legs and massage my eyes in tight concentric circles to rub out the red so I can zoom into work by 8 and slip behind my computer and appear to function productively when I will actually be screaming with a dehydrated brain and a snare-drum headache and the beatific smile of a man who drank Vitamin V and inhaled lines of cocaine from Flynn's six-pack abs at 3 in the morning before pulling my tongue down the line of hair that begins at the base of his pecs and feathers toward his pleasure zone.

It's midnight on a Thursday and I'm in the back of a sedan and we're looking for coke. I'm with Flynn and his sister and the sister's boyfriend and a guy visiting from Atlanta. His name is Justin or Jason and he looks like a coroner's photograph from a crime scene: pale eyes that broadcast bad news, bruises on his cheek, and an attitude that could wound even the dead. He keeps turning around to tell me that he thinks Kansas City is a figment of nobody's imagination. He laughs every time he says the line, like it's a hilarious and original comment about this Midwestern wasteland.

"I know Kansas City isn't as cool as Hotlanta," I say, dragging the moniker for the Georgia metropolis out like a stripper's boa. "You'll just have to put up with us for the night. We can get you on a Delta flight first thing in the morning."

He swivels in the front seat, displays the erect middle finger of his left hand, and says, "Fly this."

It's going to be a long night.

I'm going to need the coke.

And a lot of patience.

———

There are medical tests, psychological tools, and scientific schemes to determine if someone is an alcoholic. One test is the Chem 20, also known as the SMA20, also known as the sequential multichannel analysis with computer-20, also known as the SMAC20, also known as a clever collection of chemical tests performed on serum, which is also known as the remaining portion of blood once the cells are removed.

I choose not to investigate the Chem 20. I decide to conduct my own collection of tests, although far less clever and

scientific than the series of sequential multichannel analyses
with computer.

I avoid computers and medical labs and attractive, highly paid professionals wearing starched white coats that
match their starched white faces. For my tests, I employ a
random series of car accidents, late night phone conversations that resemble transcriptions of imagined alien dialogue,
and prolonged trauma to my interior organs and my epider-
mis using blunt objects, broken glass, and blinding stupidity.

———

"He didn't mean any harm," Flynn says. "He just got too
high. You know how that goes."

He's trying to defend the rude remarks made the night
before by the visitor from Georgia. I'm not interested. I roll
over and look at the bookcase next to my bed. My eyes roll
lazily from one image to the next. Ellen's passport picture
nestled inside a Plexiglas frame with my picture taken on
Jack and Karin's boat moored off Fire Island. A torn Trojan
wrapper. A Bunnykins coin bank shaped like a book. A bottle of Wet.

"I'm hungry." Flynn pokes my ass with his knee. "Let's
get breakfast."

"I have to go to work," I tell him, swinging my legs onto
the floor and sitting on the edge of the mattress. "There are
bagels in the kitchen if you want to eat. Or you can stay here
and sleep."

My eyes burn. The house music from Atlantis echoes
between the pieces of gravel that fill my head. Thinking:
How am I going to function at work?

Shower. Shave. Dress. Back into the bedroom to say
good-bye to Flynn, but his muted snore announces his return
to paradise. I kiss my fingers, touch them lightly to the foot
that extends from beneath the blue wool blanket, head to

work. Thinking: *I have to stop drinking so much during the week. This is not going to be a good day.*

Driving to work, I listen to New Order, fumble for an Altoid to mask the seemingly permanent Vitamin V breath, search for the money I thought I'd stuffed into the ashtray when we got back to my apartment after leaving Atlantis. No money. A card with a name and number. Thinking: *From what bar? What night? Who is Rory?*

At work I smile and make conversation and fill my coffee cup and walk slowly down the hall to my cubicle. The gray walls and gray cubicle sections and gray filing cabinets and gray carpeting are perfect for a day like today. No bright colors. No loud sounds. Absolutely no surprises.

I'm sipping my coffee, trying to breathe with regularity, wondering when I met Rory. I start thinking about the employee newsletter I need to write, the training manual that lies unfinished on the shelf. I hear fabric rustle, a dramatic, loud sigh, and my boss materializes above the edge of my cubicle wall. She chirps a greeting at a volume just centimeters below deafening. She's wearing a dress that features a print fabric reminiscent of a Sherwin-Williams store after an earthquake. A Technicolor fashion nightmare.

"Are you ready for your review?" she squeaks. Sharp tones slash my eardrums. "We can meet in my office. If you're ready."

I'm ready. Of course I'm ready. I can smile and nod, sharing ideas and offering comments. I can pretend to be present, though my mind is a million miles away, cradling a cocktail, nursing a nightmare. During the hourlong review, my boss covers me with kind words and compliments. She tells me I'm doing a great job. Everyone loves me. I'm such as asset to her team.

Instead of creating a warm murmur of pride and confidence, the gracious phrases make me worry. *Does she know I'm unraveling? Can she see the white heat in my eyes, the*

burning embers of fear and loathing? Will this fragile world
fall apart before I can find a permanent escape?

During the drinking years, there are many victims:
romances, friendships, professional connections, personal
faith. The Vitamin V and beer and wine and scotch and soda
seep into the infrastructure, fissures appear, holes are not
mended. One of the primary victims in the drinking years is
my liver.

This happy little internal factory, designed to clean and
process and dispense, is threatened and compromised by con-
tinuous alcohol intake. When an alcoholic pummels his liver
with the perpetual Chinese water torture of drink after drink
after drink, the internal factory is in danger of a permanent
work stoppage.

The medical community has crafted another clever collection of tests to evaluate how well the liver is functioning
at any given moment in time. The tests used most frequently
to measure liver function sound like a collection of govern-
ment agencies and garage bands: AST, ALT, bilirubin, LDH,
GGT, and total protein.

I walk into Café Sebastianne around noon. It's my
favorite restaurant for lunch, a stunning bistro housed in an
angular room in one corner of the Kemper Museum of
Modern Art. There are a dozen occupied tables, men and
women wearing business suits and serious expressions. In the
corner, near the sculpture of a heavyset waitress made from
shards of crimson-colored tile, two older women sit with
matching glasses of white wine and pained masks of societal
elegance.

Robert invites me to sit at a table near the windows that look onto the walled patio. A water sculpture, mounted on the north wall of the courtyard, splashes noiselessly as I stare through the glass.

"Sorry I'm late."

I look at my watch. It's 1 o'clock. Flynn is absolutely on schedule, his impeccable record for timeliness and taste intact despite his protestations of tardiness.

"How are you?" I say as he slips into one of the uncomfortable white plastic chairs. "Did you finish the proposal? The one you were working on?"

A big smile informs me he completed the project and met the client's deadline.

During lunch, Flynn tells me about his morning, a three-hour marathon conference call with a banker in Minneapolis, a pair of architects in Pittsburgh, an airline pilot in Las Vegas. The group was finalizing details for their next circuit party in South Beach, and Flynn lovingly covers every item they discussed, including condom colors, the drug menu for the weekend, a code word to signal which man they would target for their next group scene.

"Sure you can't come?"

I shake my head. Thinking: *I can barely navigate the trip from my apartment to the office without getting lost. How could I possibly collect my wits for a trip to Florida?*

"You've been really distant lately." Flynn sips his raspberry iced tea, licks his lips, and smiles. "I think we need to talk."

"About what?" I ask the question even though I know the answer. "What's wrong?"

"Everything is wrong."

From there Flynn tells me he doesn't have time to nurse me when I'm hungover and that he's tired of worrying about me when he calls and there's no answer and that he keeps hearing these disappointing stories about my behavior at the

Dixie Belle on a Tuesday night with the young guy from the tanning salon—or the bartender or the muscleman or whomever else I might have encountered on one of my regular drunken spins through the dark night.

Finally, after explaining why I'm a complete and total waste of his energy, Flynn tells me we should spend less time together. I suggest that the amount of time we spend together should be zero.

"And you have a good day," I say. "Have a good fucking time in Miami. I'm sure you and the other girls will be fabulously successful in getting as fucked-up as possible and fucking as much as possible."

Flynn glances nervously at the next table. "Would you please lower your voice?"

I'm ready to leave. I've had enough. My head feels like it will explode any minute, sending splattered brain matter across the paintings on the nearby wall. Without another word, I stand and pull a twenty from my back pocket.

"Thanks for lunch," I say. "Thanks for everything."

———

A glass of Vitamin V. A bottle of beer. A shot of tequila.

When consumed in measured amounts and coupled with responsible behavior, alcohol can be a delightful addition to a dinner, an evening out, a sporting event, a family reunion, a high school reunion, a college reunion, a marriage celebration, a birthday, a holiday, and a million other gatherings or activities generally referred to as special events.

A bottle of Vitamin V. A case of beer. Twenty shots of tequila.

Slam the stuff down in enormous quantities, skip the responsibility factor, and alcohol can be a loaded pistol placed snugly against the temple—or a hand-tooled Italian leather belt looped carefully over a shower curtain rod or a sharp razor blade or any other device that can kill, maim, or disfigure.

A glass of poison. A bottle of toxic resin. One hundred shots of death. Alcohol contributes to more than half of all accidental deaths and almost half of all traffic fatalities. Nearly one half. Almost 50%. In addition to the accidental deaths and deaths on roadways, alcohol is a factor in a large percentage of suicides.

A glass of Vitamin V. A bottle of beer. A shot of tequila.

Sounds almost romantic.

Almost.

———

I walk through Loose Park on a humid, still evening. The jogging path is crowded with runners and single people walking their dogs and couples pushing small children in strollers. We share the same air and physical plane, but I am disconnected from their world. I am a first-draft character in an unfinished novel; a first name, the bare bones of a life, the illusion of existence.

I am not here.

I am alone.

Thinking: *What am I going to do about Flynn? Why do I care about Flynn? I have Dylan. Dylan doesn't know about Flynn. And Flynn never knew about Dylan. It's a perfect world; I can control these elements and build something better tomorrow.*

For tonight, I'm going back to Mercier Street.

I'm going back to Mercier Street with a pair of Benjamin Franklins and an attitude for freedom, free will, free fall.

And no one can catch me.

———

If an individual has a life-threatening disease, would he seek treatment?

In most cases, yes. But that is not true with the disease of alcoholism.

Question: What percentage of the men and women addicted to alcohol seek treatment?

Answer: Less than 20%.

It doesn't take a genius to do the math. More than 80% do not get help.

This is one of the rare instances where it is better to be in the minority.

———

I drop the quarter on the pavement. *Ping*. And it's gone. Search my pockets for another, feed it to the phone, dial Flynn's number. His machine clicks on after the second ring.

"Hey, this is Flynn. I'm not homo right now, so leave a message."

He always thinks that's funny. I consider it disgusting. What if someone meaningful called?

"Flynn, this is John. I'm at QuikTrip on Main Street. I have to see you tonight. I'm coming over."

Fly through Hyde Park in hot pursuit of an ending, a finale, the last word to my first real passion since Andrew left for Denver. Yes, Dylan is pleasure. Yes, Dylan is entertaining. Yes, Dylan is attentive and intelligent and amusing.

But the passion? I've avoided the reality for months, seeking an escape with my other companion, my liquid lover. I've avoided the fact that Dylan lives his life with one foot inside our relationship and one foot headed out the door. He looks at me with one eye and glances over his shoulder with the other, constantly worried someone will discover he is gay and, oh, my Lord, involved in a romance with another man.

The passion? I've found that with Flynn. Until now. Until

this week. Until he too pulls away because he's tired of me cheating on him with a glass of wine, a bottle of beer, a shot of tequila.

Flynn's house is dark when I arrive. The drive is empty. No BMW. No Cherokee. I peer into the garage. The Jeep is inside. So it's the middle of the night and Flynn's car is gone and the house is dark and he's tired of me cheating on him and Dylan's spending the night at his parents' house and I'm so sick of this insanity.

I need a drink.

A bottle of Vitamin V. A case of beer. Twenty shots of tequila.

I need help.

———

Diseases are a package deal. They bring a host of complications, attendant risks, inherent problems. With alcoholism, the complications are numerous. They can affect internal organs, the circulatory system, brain function.

The complications associated with alcoholism include acute pancreatitis, alcoholic cardiomyopathy, bleeding esophageal varices, cerebellar degeneration, cirrhosis of the liver, alcoholic neuropathy, depression, erectile dysfunction, high blood pressure, nutritional deficiencies.

And suicide.

———

Take my pulse and my temperature. Measure my heartbeat. Connect my pressure points to an EKG. Gather the data and record it in a notebook, paint a picture of my health and well-being to document how much damage I've already done to my physical form.

Take my pulse and my temperature because those are the

only tangible elements that will illustrate the impact of 30 years of alcohol and drug abuse and sexual misadventures.

Take my pulse because you cannot take a picture of my soul.

Take my temperature because it is impossible to determine the heat that has burned my spirit.

Measure my heartbeat.

Quick. Measure it soon.

Before it stops.

9 / WRECKED

This is my world: bruises, broken promises, strained relations, ugly remarks tossed like a terrorist's hand grenades to shatter and shock.

In this world poetic phrases are misplaced or inappropriate. In this rigid world the sun does not dapple. It blazes and burns, a hard pillar of light that lays waste to my vision, cripples my view, and draws my eyes into a tight gaze as I squint to find my way from bed to bottle to a quiet corner of the room. My head is an atoll in the Pacific in 1942, exploding with unexpected ferocity, shattered by even a small, gentle sound. My throat is dry, choked with cotton and sand and granite sponges that soak up any available moisture and expand into blocks of clay and concrete.

In this world hope does not spring eternal. It evaporates in a tedious series of interconnected moments. Faith and trust and alliances of comfort and compassion do not thrive. They fail from a lack of nourishment and care. Lies are cherished currency, the medium of exchange that erases obligations, expectations, responsibility. In this place, with its scent of death and its disconnection from reality, lies are all I have to shield myself from the truth.

In this world truth does not set you free. It enslaves and captures and weakens. In this place, where the sun illuminates failure and hopelessness maintains an unremitting hold on the heart, I am lost. I am abandoned, forsaken by the man who spoke words of love and devotion, ignored by friends who choose to shield their eyes from my disintegration. In this place, with its unfinished business, incomplete acts, and a foundation of dissolving reason and claustrophobic fear, I am wrecked, broken, ruined.

This is my world: a wrecked fortress, an eroding will to live, the tattered threat of survival that blocks my path with a fierce stranglehold.

In this world the sun does not dapple.

It burns.

And I burn with it.

———

Find me. I will wait. Capture my heart. I will capture yours. Take this moment to tell me one secret. Breathe this life into your soul. Angels come when we are ready.

Find me.

———

I make a list of the reasons to quit drinking. It contains three items. The first entry is predictable, three words that echo my upbringing, societal ideals, surrender to convention: "Because I should."

The list I make of the reasons to keep drinking contains six entries. The list begins with an entry that contains four words, a statement of defiance and swagger, the conviction of a stubborn and spoiled soul: "Because I want to."

———

Sunday. Dylan leaves around 10 o'clock, the smell of our morning sex rinsed off by a shower, a protein shake for fuel, a goodbye kiss. The silence bleeds and the murmuring wind weeps.

It is our last good-bye kiss.

It is our last good-bye.

It is our last day.

At noon I consider going to Gold's. Instead, I walk down the street to Townsend Place, the 10-story condominium tower that looms above the north side of the Country Club Plaza. Dylan's friend, an anesthesiologist with his own history of drinking and drugging, asked us to feed his greyhound while he is away on business.

"Nice day, sir," the doorman says. "Beautiful Sunday morning."

I pass him and smile. "Very nice day." I cross the lobby's marble floor toward the elevator. "Good day to be outside."

Upstairs, the greyhound clatters and careens around the apartment. I open the door to the terrace, the dog slips outside for fresh air, whimpers into the wind. I sink into the overstuffed sofa in the den, click on the TV, watch CNN for a few minutes.

I perform the remaining duties when the news becomes dull. I refill the dog's food and water bowls, scatter a few extra treats on the floor, reseal the food bags and stow them safely on the counter. As I push the food to one side, I see something that is suddenly intriguing.

It is a bottle of gin. Tanqueray. More important, it is an *open* bottle of Tanqueray gin.

Don't, the wise and angelic voice says. Finish with the dog and leave. Go to the gym. Be good.

I retrieve a clean glass from the overhead cabinet, add a handful of ice, cover the cubes with orange juice that I find in the refrigerator.

Have some gin, the dark one growls. A swig. One hit. A quick shot. Fuck being good. Have a little pinch. You'll still be able to go to the gym.

I drain the orange juice and gin, say good-bye to the dog, head home to plan my next move. I head home to plan my next move because the gin is now filtering through my system and I know I'm not going to the gym, not going to buy new running shoes, not going to do the laundry.

I'm going to get lost.

Because I want to.

———

The phone rings around 4 in the afternoon. I'm on the floor in the living room, remote control in one hand, the other hand tucked behind my head.

"I got your message," Nick says when I answer. "You OK?"

"I'm good," I say, trying to remember when I called Nick. "What's up?"

He tells me that he and Elizabeth are going to a movie. He invites me to join them, but I deflect the offer with news of a migraine headache.

"It's horrible," I lie. "I'm just going to take a hot bath and then try to sleep for a while."

"Can we bring you anything?" Sweet Nick, such a gentleman, such a friend.

"No, I've got everything I need. I'll talk to you later."

When I hang up, I head into the kitchen and survey everything I need: Vitamin V, Valium, cigarettes, $40 in fresh bills, the Sunday newspaper. The simple things in life. The minor amenities. The ticket to ride.

———

When Dylan arrives around 7, I'm sprawled on the sofa. He looks down at me, frowns, sits on the ottoman without removing his jacket. I've been drinking all afternoon, small servings of Vitamin V and juice, watching television, and napping. I failed to shower or shave earlier, but the dishevelment feels natural, comfortable, correct.

"Look at you," he says, disgusted and angry. He stands, walks to the front door. "I'm going home," he tells me. "I'll see you later."

———

I'm drifting, my arms outstretched and my legs crossed at the ankle. The room is still and motionless, the silence broken only by the sound of the air conditioner's fan as it whirs and whirs and whirs.

The fan lulls me to sleep. The rest is fitful, filled with murky, incomplete dreams about Dylan and the greyhound and standing on the balcony at Townsend Place looking down at my apartment, at my street, at myself plummeting from the concrete platform and caressing the pavement below with a sloppy, permanent kiss.

I wake at 1 o'clock. Check the machine. No call from Dylan. I think about driving to his house. Decide to fix another drink instead. Stand in the kitchen, sipping the Vitamin V, swirling the cocktail in circles in the bottom of the tumbler.

In the morning I'll fix this mess, clean up this spill. Tomorrow, when I'm thinking more clearly, I'll take care of this trouble. I'll apologize and promise to never again drink and ask Dylan to forgive me.

Yeah, that's what I'll do in the morning. Tonight, I'll keep drinking. There's plenty of Vitamin V, juice, ice cubes. I've got cigarettes. No problem. Nothing to worry about. I can fix all of this tomorrow.

———

Monday. The madness bleeds through from Sunday, a vein of decay and ruin, a connection of fear, heartbreak and fever. I feel confused and thirsty and spent when I open my eyes and look at the clock. *What time is it? Am I late? Did Dylan really leave last night like an angry, bitter child?* The hands on the clock spin in circles, a blur of black and white, making it impossible for me to decipher the exact time. *Is it 7? Eight? Nine o'clock?* I roll onto my side, grab the phone, call Valarie's extension at the office and leave a message telling her I'm sick and won't be in today.

I am sick. I look at my reflection in the mirror: a man who is afflicted, unhealthy, unsound. Avoiding work and responsibility is not a choice. It is a necessity. I must find Dylan and apologize. I must find Dylan and ask for forgiveness. I must find Dylan and make him love me.

In the kitchen I survey the damage from the previous evening. Cigarette butts in the sink. An empty bottle of Absolut. A carton of grapefruit juice in a pool of tepid water on the counter. A notepad with phone numbers and names and addresses.

Watching television with a fresh cocktail: Katie Couric and Disney World commercials and the insistent tom-tom of my hangover headache playing its repetitious symphony in my head. Change the channel: CNN's talking heads chattering about world events. Another change: the Weather Channel forecasting the future likelihood of rain in Florida, thunderstorms in the Midwest, cool wind in Colorado.

Another cocktail and I'm on the phone, calling anyone, anywhere, calling Riley in New York.

"He's not here," a voice tells me. "He's supposed to be back tonight. Or maybe it's tomorrow night. Can I give him a message?"

No message. Dial another number, a friend's office in Atlanta.

"How are you?" Stephen asks. "I haven't talked to you in forever."

The sunshine pitch of his voice makes the tom-tom beat quicken and the Vitamin V slide down my throat faster. I listen to Stephen tell me about a trip he's planning, two weeks in Barcelona and a week in Madrid and a new man he met in Key West and it all sounds so fucking wonderful and beautiful and well-balanced and I hang up before he finishes a sentence about the new account he's just landed for the ad agency.

Click.

No message. No interest.

Can't he tell I'm desperate? Why didn't he listen to me? Couldn't he hear it in my voice?

I walk through the apartment, holding the phone, trying to think of someone else to call. I feel frozen, unable to leave these four rooms, a prisoner with unlimited telephone privileges and 50 cable television channels and a fresh bottle of Vitamin V and no interest in anything except finding Dylan.

Finding Dylan.

I must find Dylan.

A quick shower, a fresh T-shirt and jeans, comb my hair, and I'm out the door. I climb into the truck and head for QuikTrip. Buy a half-pint of cheap Vitamin V, a lemon-lime-flavored Gatorade, mix the two in a plastic cup. I park on a side street around the corner from the convenience store and gulp the sticky sweet poison. *Can't he tell I'm desperate?* No message. Barcelona's going to be incredible. No answer.

Leave a message. *What time is it?* They're the biggest sporting goods manufacturer in the country and it's my account. *Couldn't he hear it in my voice?*

Back on the road, I drive west toward Dylan's house. He lives in a two-bedroom rental on a tree-lined street. It's a building in need of repair and attention, and the parallel between Dylan and the place he calls home has always seemed appropriate. He rarely cleans, leaving a pile of unopened mail spilling from the table inside the front door, unwashed dishes in the sink, discarded clothes on the bedroom floor. He uses the kitchen table as his desk, and it's usually covered with papers and notes and horticulture publications and pencils and newspapers. Evidence of disarray in a life designed to be ideal and orderly. Curious. Threatening. Banished with a word and a wave and a mumbled laugh. "I'm going to clean next week," he would say occasionally. "It's such a mess."

Parked outside the mess, I can tell Dylan is elsewhere, hiding, no doubt, with a friend, the discarded daughter of the candy company baron, or with his parents. I consider driving to both locations but decide it's best to return home. It's best to go back and hibernate with my ice cubes and clear glass tumbler and the Vitamin V and a Billie Holiday CD. Let Dylan find me, I think. Let him come to my rescue, discover me as I drown in a river of tears, professing my devotion and desire to quit drinking, to get clean, to love him with a purity and grace and dedication that he's never known with another man.

Liar. I look at my eyes in the rearview mirror as I race north on Ward Parkway. They sag with fatigue and trumpet the ruined spirit that cowers within my heart. I know I've done wrong. I know I've made a terrible mistake. I know I've pushed against the boundaries with too much force this time. And I know there's no going back.

No answer. Leave a message. But there is no message.

There is only the hum of defeat, the death rattle of anguish, the knot of dread lodged in my throat and that cannot be moved by a hard flood of cool water. The tom-toms increase their rhythm and pace, pounding a bulletin of desperation and bitterness. *What am I going to do? This is all Dylan's fault. Why is he such an asshole? What time is it? Can I do anything about this?* Biggest sporting goods manufacturer. He's not here. *Can anyone help me?* Supposed to be back tonight. Fucking Dylan. If he'd listened to me last night. *Can anyone tell I'm desperate?*

I shift into third gear, punch the radio dial, tune in to NPR and listen to the broadcaster read a story about J.D. Salinger. I need medication, more Vitamin V, so I drive to Osco on Main Street, make the buy, return home, and allow gravity to continue its tenacious hold and pull me deeper into the darkness.

Deeper into the canyon.

Deeper into the only place that can give me a sense of self, of comfort, of home.

Deeper into that place that feels like death.

———

"What are you doing home? Are you sick?"

Who is it? Dylan?

"Are you OK?"

The voice. Who is it? I push the receiver into my ear and say, "What?"

"Are you sick?" It's George, a newspaper writer I met a couple of years earlier when he wrote a feature about my Internet serial. "I got your message that you were at home."

George. *Why is he calling? Did I call him and leave a message?*

"You OK?"

"Not feeling too good," I say finally. "Maybe the flu."

He offers to come over if I need anything. I tell him I'm fine, hang up the phone, drift back to sleep.

———

The second entry on the list of reasons to quit is a name: Dylan. The appearance of his name on the list is not surprising; it is reasonable at this moment of insanity. The emphasis is on someone else, not on myself. I don't include my name on the list, that I should quit drinking to save my life. It is reasonable to avoid my name because I am operating in a manner that does not involve reason. I am operating in a manner that propels me from one senseless act to the next, from one incomprehensible conversation with George to Troy's bed in Overland Park.

———

"What's going on with you?"

Troy is talking while he lights a candle, draws the blinds, loosens the bath towel that is knotted around his waist.

"Nothing." I turn over and sink my face into the pillow. Thinking: *What would it feel like to suffocate? Would I feel pain? Would I feel anything?*

Troy coats his hands with oil and begins to knead my shoulders and neck. The oil is warm, and his hands are strong and powerful. He's straddling my waist, and I can feel his warmth hanging between the cheeks of my ass. He's getting hard, and I can feel the tip of his cock as it traces the small of my back. I want to drift away, sleep, forget the crumbling world that is my life. Thinking: *Why did I come here? Why am I in bed with Troy? Why am I going to have sex with him? What about Dylan?* The questions collect in my brain even though I know the answers. I'm here because I'm desperate. And I'm drunk. I need to feel connected to someone, anyone, and Troy happened to answer when I called. I don't feel any guilt about being in Troy's bed. I don't feel any guilt about having sex with him. I don't feel any guilt, because I don't feel anything at all.

"You don't seem very happy right now," Troy says.

"I'm happy."

"You're lying."

"I'm just distracted." I reach back and caress his legs. "Do we have to talk so much?"

He squeezes my traps, sending a sharp bolt through the tissue. I know it's a good thing, that it will help stimulate the flow of blood and oxygen to the muscles, but it feels unbearable. I ask him to stop, and he squeezes harder. Then he leans down, pushing me into the mattress with his weight.

"I'll show you pain," he says. "Pain like you've never known."

———

In the dream I'm standing in a room with a man. The walls are black and unadorned. The floor is red tile. The man is looking at me. He's holding a clipboard and appears to know everything about my life.

"What are you thinking?" the man asks. "Do you want to go home?"

I nod my head. My mouth is frozen, incapable of movement.

"Do you know where home is?"

Another nod. I struggle to move my lips, but they seem connected and immobile.

"You're not going yet."

I pull my hands to my face and begin to claw at my mouth. The man scribbles notes onto the clipboard. My fingernails dig deeply into my skin. There is no blood or pain and the man shakes his head.

"Do you want to go home?" The man smiles. "Is that what you want?"

I try to speak, but my mouth is filling with blood. The blood becomes Vitamin V. The Vitamin V becomes vomit. I'm choking and my lungs are flooding and the man with the clipboard is smiling.

The man steps toward the door, reaches for the handle. He turns and smiles. "Do you know where home is?"

———

I leave Troy's around 1 o'clock with the taste of his kiss in my mouth and the swirl of Vitamin V in my heart. I'm falling faster and faster, speeding toward the ground, gravity's victim on a one-way ride to the bottom.

I feel nauseated when I get home, but the first thing I do is fix another drink. My appetite for destruction is voracious. I want to consume my future to ensure that it will not exist. I want an ironclad guarantee that this series of mistakes and lies is proof positive that I'm no good, unworthy, a walking disaster.

I need sleep, a good meal, a pair of aspirin tablets. Instead, I start looking through the CDs, pulling magazines out of the stack, rummaging through the bureau in the bedroom in search of the photographs taken in Aspen with Andrew.

Instead of the pictures from Colorado, I find a stack of old letters and magazine clippings and journal entries written in a spiral-bound notebook. I fix a fresh cocktail and curl into the overstuffed chair in the living room, surrounded by the memories and mementos. I read and drink and watch television until there is light in the east and a pounding sensation behind my left ear.

At 7 I pick up the telephone and dial my supervisor's extension at work. With a pitiful tone in my voice, I tell her that I'm not feeling well. I tell her that I'm too ill to work today. I tell her that I will call later to check in.

I tell her exactly what I've been telling everyone else during the past two days, the past three years, the past lifetime.

I tell lies.

And then I fall asleep with my head buried beneath a mountain of pillows and the telephone ringer silenced and diminished expectations that I will surface from this experience unscathed.

——

On Tuesday morning I call the office and report that I'm still in bed with this mysterious ailment. Valarie tells me to take care of myself and stay in touch. I realize that my behavior during the past two days proves that I'm incapable of both activities.

I stare at the television for an hour, transfixed with the hopelessness of being alone, of being responsible for slashing the life from my relationship with Dylan. I wait for something to happen, feeling the energy drain from my body as the sun rises higher in the sky, spilling its bright, pure light into the living room.

I walk into the kitchen around 10 o'clock, light a cigarette, pour chilled Vitamin V over fresh ice cubes. I gently sip the poison, feel it slide through my mouth and into my throat. It reignites the fire in my stomach, stoking the warm rush that races back into my body.

I wander down the hall to my bedroom, click on the computer, cruise onto the Internet. I read the news, scan the weather reports, return to the day's headlines, and imagine that these reports of events and individuals, horrors and heroism will somehow help me make sense of the disaster I've created in my life.

But they don't help. At this point I don't think anything

could help me feel better or convince me I will survive this explosion with my sanity and my soul intact. This sense of free fall is permanent.

Why care? I'm alone now, isolated from the man who had been my link to love. I am drowning, slipping further beneath the surface, bound in a suffocating, self-medicating waltz with a river of liquor, a flood of fear.

Why bother? I'm worthless. I've failed to keep my promise that I would control my drinking. I've lied to everyone I've ever loved. And I've embarked on this madness without considering the consequences.

Why me? I feel paranoid as I lower the blinds, draw the curtains, unplug the phone.

Thinking: *Please let me go.*

Hoping: *Please let me fall.*

Please let me die.

————

He is tall and slender, hesitating in the doorway while I smile and invite him inside. He takes a seat on the bench in the dining room. When he speaks there is an apologetic tone in his voice.

"I know I'm late." He glances at his watch. "I was running late from the beginning of the day. Will you forgive me?"

I hold his head in my hands and feed his lips with a hungry kiss.

"I'll take that as a yes," he says, laughing. "Have you been drinking already?"

I'd brushed my teeth and gargled with mouthwash a few minutes before he arrived, but the stale breath of my binge is inescapable.

"I had a drink after work," I say. "I mean, I only worked until noon, so I figured I'd indulge a bit. You know, it's a vacation day and all."

He consumes the lie like a trusting child. I sit beside him and we talk about his day; the client meeting this morning, the business lunch at noon. He tells me his wife is due home from Santa Fe at 8 o'clock, so he doesn't have much time.

He is a married man, the father of two children, a loving and generally faithful husband who likes to pretend he's a single gay man. He has black hair, periwinkle-blue eyes, a small nose, distinctive lips; not a classically handsome man, but an attractive man who laughs frequently. We met online, a chat-room rendezvous that began with lunch, evolved into a friendship, and included an occasional trip between the sheets until I met Dylan.

In my drinking daze this afternoon, I called his office and invited him to stop by on the way home. The call had surprised him; when Dylan and I became intimate the previous spring, I'd told him that I would no longer be available for anything more erotic than buttery-rich crème brûlée and cappuccino at lunch. It was a strange conversation that day; after several months of intimate contact, I was telling a married man that I was no longer going to participate in his duplicity.

"I thought you were being monogamous," he'd said. "Is it over with that guy you told me about?"

"Yes," I'd told him. "It's over with him. I'm feeling like a good fuck. You up for the challenge?"

My aggressive attitude was unseemly and unattractive; it was also typical of my binges. My contact with other people included volatile outbursts or boldly suggestive statements. In this case, my married friend was in the mood to be sexual, and his wife's business trip made him temporarily available.

"We should get undressed," he whispers. "I have to pickup my daughters at their piano lessons in an hour."

I want to laugh; instead, I tug at his necktie and loosen the knot. The royal blue silk gives way, allowing me to unbutton his shirt and bury my face in his chest. I draw in a deep breath, the smell of passion and forbidden lust and escape.

I am home.

I am lost.

I am drowning.

————

"I'm wrecked." The words escape my lips in a wicked whisper. I start to grin, but a smile would require too much effort and this gloomy moment demands all of my strength. My face remains frozen as I look at Christian and say, "You have anything to drink?"

Christian eyes my face, gazing at the gray smears beneath my eyes, the yellow-green glaze that adds a sickening finish to the image. "How about a beer?"

I shake my head. "Beer doesn't do any good. Is there any vodka?"

It's the middle of Tuesday afternoon, my mother's birthday, the first Tuesday in April, and I'm standing in Christian's dining room in Overland Park. I can feel the gluey spaces between the toes on my left foot. The shower I took an hour earlier erased some of the orange-juice film that coated my legs earlier in the day after I dropped a drink on the kitchen counter and it cascaded down my torso and turned my legs and toes into a sticky swamp. I ignored the mess for more than an hour as I dialed long-distance calls, drank more Vitamin V, watched the morning news programs. The filth and debris that floated in my drunken mind had been brought to life by the citrus sludge and its gummy remains.

"Yes, there's Vitamin V." Christian opens a cabinet above the dishwasher, uncaps a fresh bottle, pours an inch-deep pond into a coffee cup. "Here," he says, offering the cup. "Sip it slowly. It's too early in the day to slam that shit.

Though it looks like you've already been doing that."

"Dylan left me," I say. "He just came over the other night, turned around and that was it."

"There has to be more to the story than that," Christian says. "What did you do?"

"I didn't do anything. He just came over, freaked out, and left. I don't know what he's doing."

Christian knows my history. He's witnessed the violent outbursts, the silent withdrawals, the moments of clarity and precision between. I know I'm lying to him. He knows I'm lying to him. As usual, he avoids the obvious and swerves headlong into hedonism: liquor and lust and the exchange of one man's misery for another man's deception. It's the perfect way to waste part of the afternoon, so I settle in for a leisurely soak in Vitamin V and a languorous session in the sheets.

I don't care about anything.

Nothing matters.

I'm wrecked.

Nothing is real.

I surrender.

———

He remembers a charcoal portrait that once hung in his bedroom. A beatific baby, sleeping beneath a periwinkle-blue blanket. Tender, plump lips, delicate eyelashes, the grace and purity of a soul untouched by shame and sorrow and pain.

He wants to be the baby in the picture. He wants to sleep beneath a soft blanket, to rest without worry, to find a safe haven that is not littered with disgrace, arrogance, and fear.

He wants to be the baby in the picture, but he knows it is too late. He is ready for a farewell, a swan song, a final adieu. He knows transcendence is impossible now. He is doomed. And he surrenders.

———

The tattoo, a black ink blotch injected into smooth perfect flesh, reads JUSTIFY. I'm looking at the word, tracing the letters with my index finger, feeling the warm skin through the curtain of Vitamin V.

"Where'd you get the tattoo?"

Christian inhales, pauses, exhales. He rolls onto his back and drops one arm onto my stomach. "San Diego." He pauses, takes another deep breath. "Two years ago. After Sammy and before Martin."

In Christian's world every event or memory or reason to believe is bracketed by boyfriend bookends. He segments his life with things that happened before he met someone or after they broke up. Christian is a swirl of extroverted chatterbox and borderline lunatic. Christian is a Prada model brought to life: chestnut-colored eyes, immaculate skin, cropped black hair, a lean build that comes naturally and requires no maintenance, a job he loves, a home he tends with care, a heart that beats with passion for life. All of those elements, and a tattoo that reads JUSTIFY rides his left hip like a black-ink holster.

"I talked to Sam the other day." Christian sounds tired, dreamy, lost. "He's so happy in Dallas. And I'm so happy he's so happy."

"What's he doing there?"

"Being happy."

"I don't know anything about being happy," I say. "Now shut up and kiss me."

———

Hours later my eyes open. I am home, lying naked on my bed. I can feel the familiar stickiness between my legs, the dull ache between my ears. My apartment is dark, and I hear a voice in the living room.

"He's asleep," the voice says. "And he's earned it. You should see how much he loves to…"

I click out of the conversation, roll onto my side, stare at the wall. I want an out. I want an escape. I want to end this madness. Now I just need the right combination of chemicals to open the door to nothingness. Maybe the voice in the other room can help me arrange the elements. Maybe he can lend a hand so my scheme will succeed. Maybe he can pull the trigger for me. I'm thinking about the end of things when I realize I don't know who is in the other room. It doesn't sound like Christian. It doesn't sound like anyone I know. As I realize I don't know who's in my living room, who has apparently just pleasured himself with my body, I click back into what's being said on the phone.

"I'm leaving in a few minutes," the voice says. "I'm just going to shower and make sure he's still alive. This fucker is pretty far gone."

Yes, I'm pretty far gone.

Pretty far.

Gone.

———

I drift in, fade out, follow the liquid line through the day and into the night. I am alone now; the unnamed visitor left after a shower and a kiss on my numb and glowing lips. I remember his eyes, the smell of his cologne, the arc of his erection on my back as he pushed me into submission.

I drift in, clinging to the image of Dylan's face. I am alone now. In these rooms, this misery, the torturous realization that the mistakes I've made in the past few days are far too numerous to erase with a simple apology.

I drift in, deciding I will collect all of the pills in my possession, the chemical army of sedatives and sleeping agents, and I will wash them into my throat with the remaining Vitamin V.

Somewhere around 9 o'clock, I leave the bedroom, open the linen closet, find my secret supply of medication. I assemble the pills in a pile on a blue ceramic plate. I fill a large glass with a small ocean of Vitamin V. I take the pills, two by two, into my mouth. It takes nearly an hour to swallow the collection of tablets and capsules. I am diligent in my concentration, focused on this final combustible act.

When the last pill is deposited safely and the Vitamin V bottle is dry, I walk into the dining room. I sit at the table and write a brief note. For a writer, it is a sadly trite farewell.

"I am tired," I write on the green notepaper. "Please take care of my cat."

———

He imagines he is gone. Wrapped in a cloak of bed linen, the gentle white noise of a fan humming in the distance, he envisions himself drifting away from this world. It is his hope now to be somewhere else, to be a memory, to be a nuisance no longer to the friends and family who have witnessed his descent into a pool of pathetic and artless denial.

He imagines he will be forgiven. When he is bathed in a pure light of sorrow, his name will invoke nothing more than simple nods of recognition. "Oh, yes," they will say. "Too bad about that one. Too bad he wasn't able to keep himself above the surface."

———

I see my father standing in the corner of my bedroom. He is motionless, his pale face glowing in the darkness, his lips curved in a peaceful smile. He watches from the other side of the room, standing with his arms at his side, a statue, a memory, an angel.

I imagine that I hear him speak.

"Continue," he says. "You can go on."

When I raise myself up and lean toward the place where my father stood, he is gone. I return to the pillows, roll onto my side, close my eyes, and pray for sleep.

———

Blood pours from my mouth, pooling on the floor, the toilet seat, the bathroom sink. Pain explodes in my stomach, my throat, my head. I drop to my knees and rest my face against the cool tile wall. I'm spinning, spinning, spinning. Is it a dream? I can feel the convulsions, the tremors from within, the spasms that end with more blood and clear liquid and a ceaseless sense that I am not dying. I am destined to live in the hell of this moment, the torture of this night.

"Please let me go." My voice sounds thick and distant. "Please let me go."

———

I surrender to a fitful sleep sometime after dawn. I do not dream. I do not glide into a blissful state of rest. I hover in midair, mindful of the fact that I tried to end my life, thankful that I failed. My eyes are dry and tight when they open. I squeeze them shut and wait until I drift back into a quiet place between waking and sleeping.

When I wake at noon, I ache with the realization that I have made a disastrous mess of my life and there is to be no turning back.

Nothing matters.

I'm wrecked.

Nothing is real.

I surrender.

And for some miraculous reason, I surrender to a new sensation.

I surrender to love.

10 / Good-bye

And so I die.

On a Wednesday afternoon in April, I say good-bye to the man I've been for three decades and begin a new life. There is no dramatic pronouncement of death, no obituary seeded with sorrowful statements, academic honors, professional achievements. With the exception of a few close friends and family members, my demise goes unnoticed. I return to work, resume a daily exercise routine, reestablish the rituals and familiar patterns that demarcate the living from the dead.

As I say good-bye, everything is reversed: Black becomes white, down becomes up, despair becomes possibility. Though I have no idea yet how I will make the journey from a soulless, torn existence to a vibrant, rich life, I'm confident I will succeed. The confidence is a combination of inner strength and a newfound spirit fueled by faith and commitment. When you reach the same dead end enough times, it becomes easy to carve a new path. If, that is, you have the courage and desire to go forward without a blueprint or a guide.

———

It is late Wednesday afternoon when I wake again. I climb out of bed, pull my bathrobe from a hook on the back of the bathroom door, and wrap it around my cold, shaking body. I want to find Dylan, but since he ignored the messages I'd left on his machine during the previous two days, I dial Finn's number. Somehow I know it's time to make this call. Somehow I find the courage to admit defeat. Somehow I turn to a dear friend who will not judge or chastise. Somehow I am lucky enough to have survived my own stupidity and arrogance.

"I need help," I say when he answers. "I don't think I can make it alone."

An hour later Finn arrives with a bag of groceries and a wary expression. He's been down this road with me before. He witnessed my nine-year dry period during the second half of our 15-year relationship. He witnessed the drunken nights at the Cabaret, the excuses and hollow apologies I dispensed the past three years during my violent relapse.

"You need to eat something." Finn begins to unpack the groceries. "Roast chicken?" When I shake my head, he says, "How about ice cream? Do you think you can eat some ice cream?"

I nod and take the carton of Ben & Jerry's into the living room. I collapse onto the sofa, pull the bathrobe tighter and hold the spoon like a foreign, delicate object. It's been five days since my last meal, and the thought of food is less than appealing after consuming nothing but Vitamin V and water for so long.

"I'm afraid," I mumble. "I don't know. I don't know."

But I do know. The previous four days had been empty and oblique, but I was terrified by the thought of one day without alcohol's gentle, numbing embrace. How could I handle fear, pain, rejection? How could I ensure and sustain the rush I'd pursued for so many years? What would I do with the empty time and unfulfilled hours? I'd read about alcoholics who make the journey to sobriety. I'd heard their stories in AA meetings and television programs and documentaries. I heard them talk about acceptance, surrender, peace.

But I never thought I would share their story.

I never thought I would make the transition to a clean, sober life.

In the end, I never thought.

Until that afternoon in April, when my stomach convulsed with hunger and abuse. When the reasons I drank evaporated like drops of water on an arid plain. When the confusion and rage and loneliness and pain became so intense I knew I could surrender to sobriety and make my own journey to a tranquil life colored by honor and respect and gratitude.

My decision is made not from desperation and pain but from clarity and self-love. And though I'm terrified of living without alcohol, I know I've tasted death's permanence and I must renounce my liquid lover.

For the day.

For the night.

Forever.

———

The uncertainty of sober living is overwhelming during the first dry days. I feel aphasic and lost, unable to communicate clearly or accurately interpret simple messages and meanings. The roller-coaster rush of alcohol's embrace is replaced by suspicion, paranoia, pain, anguish. Energy drains quickly, and exhaustion is constant. Truth is a distant destination, a place on the far side of past actions and unfulfilled promises.

The life I vacated hangs behind me like a shroud, concealing the reasons I escaped and medicated and avoided. I need to find myself, to redefine who I am and reclaim the parts that remain.

Who am I?

Who do I want to be?

During my first sober days, those two questions contain the fertile seeds for future growth. And though, after years of hiding beneath a numbing blanket of deception and denial, I know that answering those two simple questions will be the first step on my path to a healthy, sane, and sober life.

I spend hours thinking about the questions. I know it will take months to sort through the debris of the past three years to begin to form an answer, but I know the basics: I am a recovering alcoholic. I am a friend. A son and brother. A survivor. I am a man who has witnessed the gradual, fragmented destruction of lives and the torment of friends who succumbed to temptation and tasted the bittersweet fruit of addiction.

And who do I want to be?

A man who is free from addiction. A man who makes responsible decisions. A man who can trust and communicate and find a way to live, love, and respect in a world that is often brittle and hard and unforgiving.

As I begin to define a future free from alcohol's ruinous embrace, I know I will have to examine my past. My drinking and romantic histories are intertwined, a soggy chronology that contains the names of men and bars and restaurants. Ticket stubs from theaters and sporting events and concerts. Photographs from botanical gardens in Tucson and restaurants in San Francisco and Long Island beaches.

When I sit quietly with the first coffee of the morning, the names and faces and facts collect in my mind. Marc was an architect. Ken was a blond with an English mastiff. David was a chef. Andrew drank scotch in his morning coffee. Tom was a banker. Brett was a financial consultant from San Francisco. There was a painter, a writer, a man who invited me to London for a weekend. I met Jack and Hugh at a party in Sag Harbor, eventually joining them for dinner in SoHo and two nights in their loft. Marc had recently returned from Brazil. David was soon to leave for Martha's Vineyard, taking his German knives and a collection of cotton aprons. The financial consultant said his wife had no idea he was sleeping with men during his business trips to New York.

I smiled. Laughed. Accepted the compliments and gifts and gracious sentiments of temporary affection. I attended the fall antiques show at the Armory on Park Avenue. I went to the opera, the ballet, opening nights of new Broadway musicals. I rode in taxis and limousines and subway cars. I flew east for Thanksgiving and Christmas, west for Memorial Day and New Year's Eve.

I danced and drank, convinced I was having a wonderful life. I met strangers who became friends as friends became strangers. I watched my bank account fade and my collection of phone numbers expand.

I declared my independence from civility with a parade of one-night stands, men who sought my company for an hour, a night, a weekend. After they left, I completed the experience with a standard ritual. I showered, changed the bed linen, poured a fresh drink, and selected suitably mournful sounds for the CD player. Melancholy music was the perfect companion to Vitamin V, and the playlist verged on a depressive's greatest hits: Joni Mitchell, Chet Baker, Billie Holiday, Lucinda Williams.

With drink in hand and a misshapen grin on my lips, I

would replay the experience in my mind. I'd speak the man's name, curving my lips to cradle the consonants and vowels. David. Patrick. Ken. Tim. Mark. Matthew. Josh. Tom. Andrew. Mitch.

The collection of monikers, a seamless list of sexual trophies, became my New Testament. The chapters created not a sensible text of history, but a disjointed description of a parade of dark, drunken nights. It contained an abundant cache of wild passion, tender deceit, and the gradually destructive abuse of one man's body and soul.

Within my New Testament, one page would carefully define the tender touch of Matt's callused hand as he held me down against the mattress, gently easing inside of me while I moaned into the crisp sheets at the Ritz-Carlton in Boston. One entry would describe a muscular visitor from Denver, a man whose name I never knew and who introduced himself at Atlantis with a firm punch to my chest before we went to my apartment and he asked me to insert my fist into his ass after he'd shaved my armpits and pubic hair. Another portion of the chaotic manuscript would describe Ken's spirited embrace when he arrived at my apartment, just off the plane from Chicago, with candid snapshots of his new boyfriend that we pored over before I began licking his neck and we tumbled into bed for a two-day sexathon.

It was an interesting existence, not unlike the lives led by my drunken comrades in Los Angeles and Dallas and Tulsa and New York and Baltimore and every other city and town across the liquor-drenched landscape of Gay America. My New Testament captured the smell of semen and sweat, the taste of Vitamin V and pain. Life became a turgid blend of events and encounters, swollen with dismay and unified with the desire to prove to myself and to those around me that I was handsome and desirable and flawless.

But during the drinking days, I was neither handsome nor desirable.

I was a fool.

I was a lunatic.

I was a lost boy.

———

And so the fool dies, the lunatic is dismissed, the lost boy is laid to rest.

On a Wednesday afternoon in April, I greet my new life with inexorable apprehension. How will I survive without liquor? Can I handle the emotions I've frozen for years with alcohol? Will I succeed in my attempt to reignite my soul and reestablish a clean, sober approach to life?

In contrast to the lonely, dark place I inhabited during my final drinking binge, my new life is something I will not have to face alone. Friends and family members offer support, encouragement, financial assistance. I'm lucky and I know it. I'm also grateful for their compassion, support, and trust.

Dylan is gone. I remain. We once shared affection, and now we share the memory of a brief moment, an incomplete love, a fragile peace. In the end, love is wicked and strong. Hope is resilient and comforting. If we keep our eyes open and our hearts clear, we can realize that life gives us adequate opportunities to experience both love and hope.

11 / Wonder

When depicted in movies or documented on the evening
news, miracles seem dramatic and astonishing. The two-
year-old boy rescued from a water-filled well after two days
of imprisonment. An elderly Mexican woman who survives
four days buried in a mountain of rubble and debris following a devastating earthquake. The single passenger who lives
when hundreds perish in a train accident. Like brilliant
telegrams from a place defined by myth and legend, these
moments of wonder defy logic, reason, and empirical
knowledge.

If it is difficult to explain the child torn safely from the
earth or the gray-haired woman who lives without food and
water, how do you describe a miracle when it occurs in your
own life? It is nearly impossible, as if recounting the experience will cause listeners to laugh with embarrassment or

shake their heads with disbelief. During the first dry days, that is my experience with some people. My miracle is nearly incomprehensible to them, as if I'm embellishing a minor incident or overreacting to a bad hangover. Only a few close friends know that the decision to choose life and the determination to succeed is a moment of unexplained beauty and unparalleled grace.

"You're so lucky," Ann says. "I had no idea it'd gotten so bad."

On a hot Sunday afternoon, we're sitting in the Classic Cup, talking over cappuccinos and the remnants of a late-afternoon lunch. As I tell my story, Ann picks at the lettuce leaves and slivers of onion on a small glass plate. I tell her about Dylan leaving, the roaring river of Vitamin V, the late-night phone calls to Los Angeles and New York. I describe the feeling of absolute terror, the shock of my truck hitting the curb as I drive drunkenly through the dark night streets in search of Dylan. I report details and emotions and the horror of realizing I had reached a curve in the road and was in danger of totally losing control.

"You are lucky," she says again. "How do you feel today?"

I finish my cappuccino. "It's not luck," I tell her. "It's more along the lines of Lazarus rising from the dead."

Ann grins. "What are you going to do now?"

"Start over." I hear the words and wonder how I'll begin. "I've made some big mistakes, but it's not the end of the world. People fuck up all the time. I've got to pick myself up and move on."

The waiter refills our water glasses and removes the pair of glass plates. I watch him walk away and listen to Ann ramble on about AA and her uncle's sobriety and a clinic in Minnesota.

"It helped him," she says. "Maybe you should think about it."

I know that I don't want to go to AA meetings or spend

time in a clinic in Minnesota. I appreciate Ann's suggestions, but I know that I need to define my own program for sobriety. I know that the stubborn and unyielding components of my personality that contributed to my alcoholism will prove invaluable as I create a sober life.

"So what are you going to do about Dylan?" she asks. "You want me to call him?"

"No," I tell her. "Bowen and Ellen called already. He was very polite but made it clear he didn't want anything to do with me. I think I'll write him a note and apologize."

"That's a good idea." Her voice softens and she shifts in her chair. "And what are you going to do about you?"

"Baby steps." I smile and light a cigarette. "Three steps forward, two steps back. It'll be one day at a time and today is the first day of the rest of my life and blah, blah, blah."

Ann laughs and suggests that we go out into the beautiful weather. We leave the restaurant and walk into the crowded streets of Westport. It's good to be with Ann. Good to be alive. And good to be sober.

The day is like a dream: a warm breeze, a cloudless sky, the muffled sound of conversations and laughter coming from the sidewalk tables at Zola and Harry's Bar. We stop at Yako Gallery, examine the artwork and picture frames and assorted gift items. We talk and stroll for an hour, and then Ann announces that she has to go home and get ready for a date.

"Ouch," she says. "Did that hurt?"

"Why should it?"

She looks at the ground. "Because of you losing Dylan. It's just so sad."

It is sad, an unexpected detour away from one place toward a new life. But I'm going to focus on getting myself clean and sober before I worry about Dylan.

Ann continues to apologize, and I tell her to have a good time on her date. With a gentle kiss on my cheek and a fluttery wave, she disappears around the corner. I retrace our steps back to the Classic Cup parking lot, climb into my truck and head for the market.

———

"John?"

I'm in the produce aisle at Sun Fresh in Westport when I hear someone say my name. I look away from the bananas and kiwi fruit. It's a man I met at an after-bar party a few days after Andrew moved to Denver. We'd flirted and traded dating stories and shared dinner a few times before tumbling into bed for a drunken night of sex and laughter. Since then we'd seen each other at bars or parties, but there had never been serious interest in pursuing anything beyond the occasional night of lust and liquor.

"Hi, Corey. How are you?"

He steps closer and touches my arm. "How are *you*?"

"Good. Just buying a few things."

"I heard what happened." He looks over his shoulder like an informant who fears detection. "I'm really sorry."

And so it begins. A murmur, an overheard remark, the drums beating between tastefully decorated dens in Armour Hills and condominiums in Overland Park and renovated carriage houses in Hyde Park. Within a few days, many of my friends hear about my alcoholic explosion and Dylan's retreat. I soon learn to face their questions with a smile and a vacant glance.

"Thanks," I say as Corey leans closer. "Guess the grapevine's already got the story, huh?"

"I ran into Sam at a party last night. He didn't say much, but I could tell it wasn't good. Are you doing OK?"

"I suppose," I say. "I'm still here, anyway."

He squints. "What's that mean?"

"Nothing. Just means I'll be fine."

"Let me know if I can do anything." Corey squeezes my

arm and smiles. "Call me next week. Let's go to lunch."

As he walks away, I start to feel nauseated and feverish. The brief encounter has brought everything rushing back: the liquor-soaked days, Dylan's angry voice on the phone, Finn's stern paternal warnings to stop the madness, the blood pouring from deep inside as I vomit for hours after swallowing the sedatives and Vitamin V. I feel like crying, but I don't want to shed tears in public. I pull the fruit from my basket, return it to the bin, feel instantly and completely alone and lost.

Some men drink from boredom, others when they fear a lover is slipping away or losing interest. Loneliness has always been one of the deadliest triggers for my drinking, and it sweeps over me as I walk through the store. I feel suddenly exhausted. And terrified. I'm on my own with nothing between me and a bottle of Vitamin V. Except one thing.

I want to live. Without liquor. Cold turkey. I've fucked up for the last time. No more second chances. The concept of weaning myself from alcohol with a methodical program is impossible. I have to stop. And I have to do it now.

I quicken my pace and head for the exit. I gaze at the floor when I pass the liquor department, averting my eyes from the bottles and neon signs and the packaged despair that wait for me like the devil's accomplice.

———

Home. Safe at home. The apartment is still and empty when I return, a tomb littered with unread newspapers, piles of laundry, pieces of unopened mail. I pace and smoke and watch the windows darken as the day drains toward night.

I have no plans, nowhere to go, nothing to do. I'm alone and I can't stop thinking about Dylan. I replay the previous weekend in my mind. We'd stayed home on Friday night, eating dinner and watching a video. On Saturday, we went to the Fine Arts to see *Waiting for Guffman*. Before Dylan had arrived that night, I'd inhaled a pint of Vitamin V straight from the bottle. The undefined anger that had boiled just beneath the surface for months had exploded when I was crossing the street to reach the ATM before the movie. A black sedan had jerked to a stop as I entered the crosswalk. A pair of women inside smirked, suggesting with their expressions that I had somehow interrupted the most important event in the history of the world. Instead of politely stepping aside, I'd kicked the car and snapped at them.

"Get the fuck out of the way."

They stared back at me, and I continued walking. Dylan was waiting, and I didn't want to be late for the movie. The evening was identical to hundreds that I'd survived during the previous three years of relapse; drink alone before anyone arrived, cloak the scent of alcohol with mouthwash and mints, stumble through the night with wild eyes and an uneven gait. Inevitably, the following morning I would remember bits and pieces of the previous day while other events, names, memories were lost forever.

The images are stark and unapologetic; frozen in my mind, exaggerated by the simple fact that it might be the last time I would see Dylan. I ache from the emptiness. I conjure his image in my mind and bury my face in the pillows where he once slept. My behavior is melodramatic and unlike my usual self, but I'm operating without a plan, moving forward without a map, and the idle hours magnify the longing I feel for both Dylan and alcohol.

At 6 o'clock, I make coffee and watch the local news. The reports are dispatches from a distant planet. I've been so out of touch with current events and contemporary issues that the news is utterly foreign and incomprehensible. As the images shift and fade and multiply, I start to feel sick again. Should I call someone? Make plans for dinner or a movie? Deflate into a sullen mass on the sofa, surrounded by the jarring echoes of the sounds of my final binge?

As I begin to pace, the apartment comes to life and its shadowy corners expose the memories of my drinking days. I hear the arguments with Andrew and the drunken phone calls to anyone who will listen. I see myself engaged in mindless sex with strangers who steal money from my wallet and years from my life. I look at the front door and see the new brass nameplate that reminds me of the night I kicked my way into my own apartment. I examine the scratches on the walls, the red wine stains on the floor.

I fall into bed and stare at the ceiling. Can I make it this time? Why should this attempt at sobriety be any different from the others? Does anyone know what this is like?

The night passes slowly. Around 8 o'clock I decide to clean. I scrub the bathroom and vacuum the floor and dust the blinds. At first it mimics mindless behavior, something to do to keep from drinking. And then I realize that it's actually the best thing to do: Clean. Get clean. Wipe away the soot and debris and start with a fresh slate.

During the next three hours, I scrub and scour and spray and dust and sweep and polish. Trash bags pile up at the curb. For the first time since I moved into the apartment, I can make sense of the closets. I arrange the books on the shelves and alphabetize the CDs. I flood the kitchen sink with bleach and soap to erase the stains left in the white enamel by cigarettes and coffee.

I clean like a madman. My speed quickens as I finish the kitchen. It's the last room, and I'm almost done cleaning when I make a disheartening discovery. I open the cabinet door to wash the shelves and there's my misery: a cache of empty, dusty Vitamin V bottles. I stop counting after twenty. Pint bottles and fifths and half-pints. I move a paint can and find three dust-covered wine bottles and assorted beer cans.

I pull the bottles and cans out and arrange them on the floor. I sit and count them again. I'm working without concentration and arrive at different totals three times. Finally I open a new trash bag and load the dirty mess inside. I fold the top, close it with a twist tie, toss the bag into the back stairwell with a resounding thud.

I want to cry, but nothing comes. It's nearly midnight and I crawl back into bed and wait for the first light of a new day.

———

When romance sours and lovers separate, there is generally a sense of closure. The farewell dinner. A final note. One more bittersweet conversation on the phone. For alcohol and me, there was no closure. There was only the echo of a trash bag filled with dust-covered bottles, the faded stains of red wine on a white wall, the silence of a good-bye never spoken.

———

The next morning, I collect the random thoughts that filled my head throughout the sleepless night. Despite the lack of rest, I feel invigorated and ready for the challenges ahead. I know I must begin my new life with a pragmatic approach. As if I am preparing for a long road trip or overseas voyage, I assess the accumulated damage, contemplate the realities of my situation, and plan for tomorrow.

I also know that I'm fortunate: My finances, physical health, and mental stability are threatened but not destroyed. My most valued friendships remain intact. I'm employed, own a reliable vehicle, remember how to tie my shoes and make coffee and buy postage stamps. Though they seem inconsequential on the surface, I know that these small nuggets of knowledge and faith will form the foundation for my new life. I know they will ground my progress and support my attempts at independence.

12 / THE ADVANTAGES OF ALCOHOLISM

"I like being drunk," Hunt says. "It makes me feel good."

"Good?" I'm surprised by Hunt's comment, considering that he's nursing a hangover on my living room floor at 3 o'clock on a Saturday afternoon. "How does it make you feel good?"

"Just makes me do things I wouldn't normally do. Let's me get outside of the box." He glances at the bulge in his boxer shorts, then he looks at me and smiles. "So to speak."

———

Advantage #1: Alcoholism is educational. During my drinking daze, I learn I can kick in the front door of my apartment while intoxicated. I learn I can physically assault my boyfriend when he accidentally says something that ignites a firestorm of rage in my frozen heart.

I learn I can lie to everyone who is important in my life. And I learn I can be tempted to consider having sex with strangers in exchange for money that I can use to buy more alcohol and cocaine. Luckily, the closest I come to prostitution is posing in a stranger's apartment in my underwear while he sits in a leather wing back chair squeezing his erection through his nylon running shorts. It was an intricate lapse in reason that started with an offer from a friend who makes his living as an escort and ended with my embarrassed departure from the stranger's apartment.

I learn many lessons, the most important of which is that I can hate myself more than I hate anyone else.

———

It's a Friday night, a dark, starless evening, three years before Hunt's visit to my apartment. It's a Friday night, the end of a night of drinking and dancing. It's a Friday night and Andrew and I are drunk. We're arguing about a mistaken comment made at the Cabaret. This is familiar ground. During the past year, we've argued and discussed and quarreled so many times that the harsh language and raised voices have become punctuation marks in our relationship.

As usual, the argument begins as a small flame of discontent. He is upset with my attitude, and my attitude is making me upset with him. I throw a rude remark. He tosses a sad slash. The flame gains momentum, burning a hole between us, widening with each hateful remark.

The violence is unexpected, an explosion that surprises Andrew and disgusts me. I swing at him with a knotted fist. He covers his face with his arms, rolls into a ball on the floor. I stand over him, screaming, spitting anger. I lean down and throw a punch. It strikes him on the side of his face. Another blow. Hate and anger spill from my mouth, a lava flow of insanity and rage that covers Andrew and chokes my heart. I feel powerless and confused, a mad marionette pulled by invisible strings from above.

I continue to swing. Andrew runs into the bedroom. I follow him with a trail of shouted obscenities and mute disgust. During the next few minutes, I strike Andrew and curse his name. For some reason, I grab a pile of his clothes and carry them into the hallway, intending to throw them into the street. Andrew closes and locks the front door. In a rage that springs from a dark place deep within my wounded heart, I lurch toward the door and kick it open with a ferocity that embeds the door handle in the interior wall.

There is a momentary silence. We're both so stunned that we cannot speak. A few minutes later, when we return to the living room, there is a knock on the front door. A man's voice filters through the wooden barrier.

"This is the police," the man says. "Is everything OK in there?"

———

Advantage #2: Alcoholism is portable. I can drink anywhere. I can drink in my apartment: the living room, the bedroom, the bathroom, and the kitchen.

I can drink in my truck: driving to work, driving home from work, driving down the interstate on the way to visit my mother for the weekend, waiting in the drive-through lane at Kentucky Fried Chicken, waiting for the light to change from red to green.

I can drink at work: small sips from a half-pint of Vitamin V, a shot of scotch in my morning coffee, a beer in the bathroom stall.

I can drink at social gatherings: a bottle of chardonnay at a baptismal celebration for a friend's daughter, eight cosmopolitans at a pool party in Westwood, four bottles of

Guinness at a birthday dinner, innumerable shots of Vitamin V at a farewell reception for a coworker.

I can drink on airplanes: miniature bottles of Vitamin V, inexpensive white wine in plastic cups, beer, and champagne.

I can drink in public: restaurants, sporting events, theater lobbies during intermission, clubs, cocktail lounges, and piano bars.

I can drink in private: Hell can be found anywhere that I am alone.

———

Hunt is a former drinking mate, someone I met at an after-bar party a few months before I quit Vitamin V. He came by somewhere between 3 and 4 this morning, rang my doorbell, asked if he could sleep on my sofa. He lives in the suburbs south of Kansas City, and the drive home seemed daunting. Of course, most basic tasks seem daunting after you've consumed as much alcohol as Hunt does on a normal night out.

Even though Hunt and I no longer hit the clubs together, we talk every few weeks, late-night telephone conversations when he's getting ready for another night at the Cabaret and I'm getting ready for bed. I respect his choice to drink, because he knows—and follows—his body's limit with alcohol. He respects my choice to remain clean. Our friendship may appear odd and unbalanced to some of my sober friends, but I like Hunt and pray that he will one day seek a sober place in the world. In the meantime, I'll let him spend the night on my sofa if it means he's not driving under the influence. I'll let him use my bathroom the next morning to shower and shave with a head that aches and clatters. And I'll also let him engage me in conversations that celebrate his choices.

"I hate feeling bad the next morning." Hunt rolls onto

his side and rests his head against the ottoman. "But I love feeling good the night before."

———

Advantage #3: Alcoholism is liberating. Drinking allows me to engage in unprotected sex with unfamiliar men. It also eliminates my inhibitions so I mistreat everyone who crosses my path, including the man I love, the mother I respect, the man I wish I could become. It makes me feel free.

———

"Your neighbor heard a disturbance," the police officer tells me when I open the door. "Everything OK?"

There are two officers, two men dressed in dark blue uniforms sent to serve and protect. I tell them everything is fine. I tell them there was an argument. I tell them I appreciate their concern.

"We need to make sure she's OK," the first officer says, trying to peer behind me, trying to see into the apartment.

It takes a brief moment before I realize that the men in the hallway, the men dressed in blue, the men who are here to protect me from some unknown harm believe that I have been arguing with a woman. I'm fitfully drunk, but my mischievous sense of the absurd surfaces without effort.

"Oh," I say, smiling. "He's fine. We're both fine."

The two men share a bemused glance. They smile back and the first officer says, "Well, we need to make sure *he* is OK."

———

Advantage #4: Alcoholism is easy to learn. Drinking excessive amounts of alcohol can be accomplished without guidebooks, college courses, private tutors, instructional pamphlets, motivational speakers, teachers, tenets, or rules.

———

When Hunt was 22, his father hit him with such force during a drunken argument that Hunt's nose was destroyed. It was later rebuilt by a skilled plastic surgeon in Dallas. I remember hearing the story one afternoon at Margarita's on Southwest Boulevard. Hunt's voice sounded slow and frozen.

"My dad was a good man," Hunt had said, his eyes as flat and dull as the gaze of a stillborn baby. "He didn't mean any harm really. I think he just didn't know how to show he loved me."

———

Advantage #5: Alcoholism is eternal. As I prepare to celebrate my third sobriety anniversary, I realize that some wounds will never truly heal: the scar on my left bicep, the imbalance in my vertebrae, the fragmented memory, a heart that is haunted by fractured relationships and failed attempts to save itself from certain death.

———

"I love you," I say to Andrew the next morning. "I'm sorry I hit you last night."

The apartment is still and quiet. The front door is held in place by a chair tucked beneath the knob. We plan to go to a hardware store later to buy a new lock and deadbolt. If we repair the damage ourselves, the landlord will be unaware that I gained entry by kicking the door open with a violent and alien force. We are more concerned with the physical harm done the night before than the invisible damage to our hearts, minds, and spirits. It is a pattern, a path, a predictable element of our relationship, and we stumble forward into the future without opening our eyes.

"I know you're sorry." Andrew smiles. The bruises are barely visible on his boyishly handsome face. "I love you too."

———

Advantage #6: Alcoholism is painless. On most evenings, I consume so much Vitamin V that I am completely numb. I can't feel pain. Of course, I can't feel pleasure either. But life is about compromise, and I'm willing to negotiate if it means I can escape from the world and drown in my own private misery. This, I believe, is the greatest advantage of alcoholism.

13 / Damage

He looks in the mirror every morning, searching for signs of change and promise, gazing into his twin's brittle blue eyes. He hopes the damage is repaired, prays he was miraculously repaired during the night.

The prayers go unanswered. The damage will be healed, but it will take years. These fissures are not erased in a moment. They are too deep to disappear with a hope or a prayer. They require concentrated effort, a fervor and force that comes only through the repetition of sane, sober living. The love of self is completely foreign to him until one morning when he looks in the mirror and realizes that the damage isn't the important thing.

The important thing is healing.

And healing is something he can learn to do. One day at a time.

———

"How you are, buddy?"

Riley sounds elated when he calls in the middle of the night. I'm in bed with a visitor, a man named Nathan who appeared in my line of sight at a restaurant in Leawood when I was waiting for Hannah to finish her shift waiting tables. Nathan rolls over and mumbles into the pillow as I carry the telephone into the bathroom.

"I'm doing fine," I tell Riley. "How you be?"

Riley is also fine. He and his wife are in Texas, business meetings in Houston, a weekend in Austin with friends. I met Riley when I worked in New York. In the 10 years since then, I've heard him talk about his struggles with addiction. Never life-threatening, always just a thin layer of ice with the potential to crack and allow him to plummet into an icy abyss of denial, retreat, agony. Even though I'm once again battling the bottle myself, I pretend that all is well, life goes on, the future looks bright. Riley tells me that he and Beth are thinking about having a baby, considering the consequences of adding another passenger to Planet Earth. The news is surprising. Besides disclosing his struggle with alcohol, Riley once confided that he was confused about his true sexual direction. He and Beth were high school sweethearts. He couldn't stand the thought of disappointing her—or their parents—so he agreed to a wedding when she proposed the year after they graduated from college. Some people select comfort and familiarity instead of truth, pretending that their choice will magically replace fiction with fact.

"If it's a boy," Riley says over the line in the middle of the night from Texas, "we'll call him Ian. That's the Irish version of John. What do you think? It's our way of honoring your recovery."

Wonderful. Riley and Beth plan to name their first son

after a man who can barely draw his daily bath, who stands surrounded by the debris of a shattered love affair, who finds it difficult to imagine what it will be like when his namesake is born.

"That's very cool," I tell Riley, unsure of what other reply would make sense. "Thank you very much."

————

My thoughts are murky and random. There is no rhythm, only a series of disconnected blips and bleeps that resemble a Jackson Pollock painting or a dozen eggs dropped from a second-story window onto a gravel sidewalk. I listen to Mozart arias in an attempt to relax, burrowing beneath the emotion and elemental beauty of Cecilia Bartoli's voice in lieu of tranquilizers.

The damage is everywhere and unanswered questions hang in the air, overripe fruit that has been ignored for too long and will soon expire. Why am I depressed? I am luckier than most; I survived.

————

Damage comes in many forms, consuming its victims with different appetites and devices. Candy is bulimic. I drink Vitamin V and orange juice before work in the morning. Jan steals Tommy Hilfiger shirts from department stores. Colin smokes too much. I stop home at lunch to slam a pair of Dewar's shots. Daniel gambles at Harrah's until his checking account is dry and his wife leaves him for a Williams-Sonoma sales clerk. I drink a bottle of chardonnay as I dress for a dinner party that will inevitably include more wine and delicate glasses filled with liqueurs. Jules mines the medicine cabinets in his friends' apartments to replenish his supply of Valium when the doctor refuses to refill his prescription because

Jules is unable to make a one-month supply last longer than two weeks.

Damage comes in many forms.

Damage is everywhere.

Damage consumes its victims.

14 / Ghosts

Every life has elements of mystery and intrigue. Interlocking conversations separated by years, time zones, expectations. The unexplained kiss shared with a stranger on a subway platform in the hours between midnight and dawn. Found objects that are lost to another when property is divided at the end of a relationship. Friends who fade from view and inhabit dream sequences, ghosts hovering in the distance like tissue-paper prophecies, moving with silent grace, disturbing everything and nothing all at once.

——————

I make lists of the reasons I'm an addict. The list is filled with fingers pointing at my parents, my siblings, the deep grooves of shame and sadness and insecurity that nearly split my heart.

I'm an addict because I was raised by parents who were raised by alcoholics.

Because I was raped at a young age by an older boy in the neighborhood.

Because it's a pattern of escape that pleased my fragile heart and emboldened my frightened soul.

I'm an addict because I fear failure.

Because I fear success.

I'm an addict because I'll never have what I'll never want.

Because I'm shy, afraid, unwilling to take risks without random shots of artificial courage.

I'm an addict because I am powerless when it comes to alcohol.

Because hope is hard to find in a world that feels empty.

I'm an addict because I want to be an addict.

Because I feel worthless, weak, wounded.

I make lists, study the entries, add and subtract the reasons and symptoms and worries that combine to create a stark landscape of hopelessness, escape, avoidance, denial.

I am an addict.

The reasons are many. The symptoms multiply. The worries swirl around my ankles and threaten to rise above my head, to suffocate me in a sea of sorrow and tragedy and pain.

I am an addict.

Because.

I make lists as a point of departure, a beginning for my recovery. The lists are important tools for my new life. As I write entries in my journal and document my thoughts about the forces that propelled me into active addiction, I begin to see the patterns that began long before I was born. Patterns that continued during my childhood, lessons that taught me to use alcohol as a weapon, a cocoon, a source of pleasure and courage. I watched the adults in my family, our neighborhood, the restaurants where we dined on Saturday nights, everyone of a certain age, drink with pleasure. I watched and I learned and when I reached a certain age, I tasted the power and pleasure and discovered that alcohol could free my mind from the pounding drum of insecurity and fear.

During my 10th summer, I learned to drink. I learned to run. And I learned to bury my wounded heart in a shallow pool of alcohol. The lessons I learned during my 10th summer created the patterns that appeared in every entry on my list. I am an addict because I learned to be an addict. I am an addict because I learned that life was easier when I allowed alcohol to control my destiny without my direct involvement. I am an addict because I learned to be an addict.

I am an addict.

Because.

————

He is older, perhaps six or seven years older. I am 11. He is my friend's brother. His name is Aaron, and he overwhelms me. I dream about him at night and tell him that I like him more than anyone else, and he returns the affection with wrestling matches beneath the brown plaid wool blanket that covers his bed. He wraps his arms around my chest, pushes his mouth to my ear.

"Tell me that you give up," he says, warm breath and wet lips. "Tell me that you surrender."

I always surrender. He is older, and I am infatuated with him, even though I will not know how to define the sensation until I am Aaron's age. We wrestle. Aaron shows me how to navigate a narrow pathway above Indian Creek on my bike with the red vinyl banana seat and the playing cards that click a metronome's rhythm in the spokes. The beat matches the meter and measure of my heart whenever I'm with Aaron.

The perception of attraction to another male first appeared the summer before Aaron's family moved to our neighborhood. An older man was living for a few weeks with his sister and her husband in a house on our street. He was blond, he wore white T-shirts and faded jeans, and he washed his car every Saturday afternoon. I would walk by and watch from the corner of my eye, not knowing why I was keeping this stranger under surveillance. Once or twice he noticed me walking on the opposite side of the street. He'd wave and smile, and my stomach would ricochet through my body with excitement.

At night I'd hide in my bed, safe and secure under my Snoopy sheets. I would conjure a vivid and detailed image of the blond man. I would clearly see the white T-shirt hugging his back and flapping in the breeze as he doused his red Camaro with the garden hose. I pictured the jeans, the curve of his thigh, the way he smiled and waved when I walked down the street.

I didn't know why, but I somehow decided this vision and its attendant pleasure would be my summer secret. At the time I imagined it would be a singular event, a private glimpse into an adult world, a glimmer of life on the far side of childhood. It was only years later, as I retraced the steps that took me from the suburbs of Kansas City through an active and varied life as a gay man, that I realized that those two summers of my youth played an indelible role in every choice I made from my 10th year until the spring following my 39th birthday.

———

Everyone knows. The secretary on the elevator who talks about the fresh vegetables she bought at the farmer's market. A small boy holding an ice cream cone as he waits for his mother to finish her phone call near the A|X store.

Eric, the waiter with the almond-shaped eyes and mocha skin who refills my coffee and entertains our table with tales of his adventures in Milan and Dallas. My mother in Florida and my sister-in-law in Connecticut. The taxi driver in TriBeCa. A friend who calls late at night when I've been drinking all day.

They know.

Why don't I?

Their faces shift and slide through my consciousness. Vapors of memory and mischief, elusive messengers who deliver empty and invalid packets of information.

I watch them as they watch me. They're searching for signs of abuse and dismay. I present a smile, a wink, a nod of recognition. I invite their scrutiny, offering solid alibis and substantial proof that I am innocent.

Until proven guilty.

They know.

Why don't I?

I was born guilty.

That was my crime.

————

The sun drenches Aaron's shoulders with radiant light. We are riding our bikes through the neighborhood, spinning wheels, in a competitive spirit, with the rhythmic clatter of the playing cards on my wheels. Aaron turns his head, tossing instructions and taunts over his shoulder like a coach, a brother, a tease.

"Faster!" he shouts. "Don't be a pussy."

I pedal more quickly, gripping my handlebars with excitement and fear.

"Turn here." He fakes to his left and then careens to the right. "Not left, idiot."

I follow him onto an unpaved road, the gravel and dirt

shooting from beneath my tires like bullets and shrapnel. He arcs along the unfinished street, making lazy loops with his 10-speed. I watch his legs as they pump the pedals and he stands up from the narrow black seat. I feel older when I'm with Aaron, like his peer or a colleague, even though he ignores me if he sees me when he's with his friends. I tolerate the dismissals because I know he will eventually invite me up to his room for another wrestling session beneath the brown plaid blanket.

"Come inside." He calls to me from the front porch of a house that's under construction. "I want to show you something."

I drop my bike and scramble up the clumps of dirt and gravel that lead from the street to the house. I hear Aaron walking through the house, the thunder of his steps on the plywood flooring, his whistle echoing through the empty, incomplete rooms. I follow Aaron into the house, listen for the sound of his voice. I hear only the wind racing through the rafters of the unfinished roof. I take a few steps forward, toward the back of the house. I call Aaron's name. There is no reply, only silence, only the sound of the wind against the unprotected wood.

As I walk around a corner, I feel a hand on my arm. Aaron pulls me toward a wall. He pushes my chest into the dry wall, rips my shorts down, leans into my ear and whispers.

"This will feel good," he says. "Just relax."

———

The ghosts leave behind gifts and mementos and slivers of memory. A white ceramic coffee cup from Pottery Barn. Pictures taken in Tucson and Phoenix and Flagstaff. Newspaper clippings about a trip to Alaska and an envelope of materials from a writing resource center. A recipe for chicken vegetable soup. Ticket stubs to a Craig Lucas play.

Teabags from Seattle and a half-filled bottle of Aveda hair gel and the name of a masseur in Aspen.

I accidentally break the white ceramic coffee cup on a cloudy, damp day in December. I seal the pictures from Arizona in a manila envelope and bury them in the bottom of my bureau drawer. I discard the newspaper article about Alaska and the writing resource information one morning in August. I send the recipe for chicken vegetable soup to a friend in New York. The Craig Lucas ticket stubs serve as bookmarks, though they will become lost and forgotten in the years to come. The tea from Seattle is delicious, and the hair gel is aromatic and useful. I forward the masseur's name to a friend in Boulder.

There is order and balance in a well-manicured life, and I sense that I will maintain my balance without the trinkets and trifles presented in a moment of artificial passion and ardor. Of course, I keep a few select items: a trio of gold rings, a pair of bedside tables, a collection of porcelain rabbits, a Bugs Bunny wristwatch. These items and the men who offered them in love and faith will forever have a home in my heart, while the ghosts will fade into a fine mist and eventually vanish into emptiness.

———

A trail of terror runs through my heart. Aaron is angry. He is yelling, his voice exploding in my ear like a violent kiss.

"Why did you tell him?"

Aaron is angry. I told his brother about the afternoon in the empty house. I told his brother that Aaron had violated me. I told his brother that it hurt and I didn't like it and it made me feel bad.

"Are you fucking insane?"

Aaron is angry. I confessed everything to his brother one day when we were walking home from school.

"I can't believe you could be such a baby."

I told his brother that Aaron had forced himself inside of me, that he had made me bleed. And now Aaron is angry.

"God," he screams in my ear. His mouth turns into my face, spit stinging my burning flesh. "You are such a faggot."

———

I want to tell my boyfriend. I am 18. He is older, maybe three or four years older. He is my friend, an ally to trust and love and challenge. We met outside of a bar in downtown Kansas City, a wet and damp winter evening when my parents were out of town and I was out of excuses. I wanted to taste gay life. I'd read about it and heard about it and fantasized about it. Now it was time to submerge myself in male affection and comradeship and sex.

"Can I tell you something?"

We are in his apartment, knotted together like a living pretzel, wedged tightly together between ambitious lust and admirable affection. I draw my tongue along his lips. I am trying to unlock something, to detect how he might react if I tell him about Aaron, about the rape.

"Yeah," he says. "You can tell me anything."

"What if it's something bad?"

"Anything." He kisses me lightly, brushing his plump lips over the dimple that dots my chin. "It's important that we trust each other. Tell me that you trust me."

I start to speak, my mouth opens and the air escapes and I try to breath and nothing happens. I struggle to form a word, to find a sentence, to speak.

"Well?"

I find a smile, an empty smile. "It's nothing," I whisper. "Let's go to sleep."

———

Shame. I feel shame and embarrassment. I trusted Aaron. I believed him. I wanted him to be happy, to make me happy.

And he did.

Until that day.

"You are such a faggot."

When I leave the house, I follow any path that avoids Aaron's house. In school his brother eyes me suspiciously. Our friendship grinds to a halt, screeching and skidding into a heap on the side of the road.

Shame. I feel shame and disappointment. I trusted Aaron. I believed him. I wanted him to teach me about baseball and soccer and playing guitar. I wanted to be his friend. I wanted to make him happy.

And I did.

Until that day.

"You are such a faggot."

———

The therapist is a middle-aged man with cotton-candy hair and Buddy Holly glasses. He smells like mint and cigarettes when he opens the door to his office and waves his arm toward the leather chaise or the chintz sofa.

"Sit wherever you'll be more comfortable," he says. "Can I get you a cup of tea?"

"No, thank you." I choose the rocking chair in the corner. "I just had something to drink. I'm fine for now."

We talk about the weather, his new country house, my weekend plans. Then he says, "So how are you this week?"

"I'm fine." I want to tell him about Aaron. I've been having violent flash dreams of my childhood for the past month, and I want to decode their meaning. I start to tell him, but my throat implodes. I can't talk about it. Can't tell him. Can't speak about the shame, even though it's 20 years later and I'm safe inside this office in a high-rise on Manhattan's upper west side.

"So everything's going well?" He pushes the Buddy Holly glasses up his nose with the thumb of his right hand. "You've had a good week?"

A smile, a polite statement about my progress, another smile. I don't want to talk about the ghosts. I don't know how to talk about them. I've spent two decades holding them inside, keeping the secret buried beneath my jovial grin and even-tempered disposition.

"Yes," I say, picturing Aaron's face and remembering the taste of his kiss. "I've had a great week."

During the remainder of the session, I evade the issue. The picture of Aaron flickers and fades, the feel of his hands on my waist evaporates, the scent of his sweat dissolves until there is nothing in view except a middle-aged man with cotton-candy hair and Buddy Holly glasses.

After a few quiet minutes, the therapist checks his watch and smiles. "I think we're moving in the right direction," he says. "I'll see you next week."

———

Ten years later, I am ready to tell my story. I never shared the shame of Aaron raping me with anyone. Until now. As a sober man, I am ready to recapture the part of my heart that Aaron removed with his callous and selfish desire. I wanted to please him. He wanted to please himself. It was the perfect recipe for control and manipulation. Aaron raping me on that afternoon so many years ago was one of the key elements to my identity as a gay man.

My parents never discussed sex. I learned about sex from my friends, from the pornographic picture books I discovered in my older brother's bedroom. I gazed at the pictures, at the naked men and women linked by erections and lust. Staring at the copulating couples was titillating in the beginning, but I soon realized I was more aroused by the men in the magazines. I wanted to know about their bodies, the pillars of hard flesh that towered from between their legs. I fantasized about being their partner, about feeling them drive deep into my body with volatile pleasure. I didn't have a name for the feeling, but I knew then that it would be my destiny.

He feels the secret burning in his heart. A time bomb with a slow fuse, a long memory, the potential of an enormous explosion just beneath the surface. He hears the timer, the soft ticking from some dark crevice a million miles away. He feels the heat as the fuse glows, the subtle scent of burning flesh and death and his own dark secret.

He considers another therapist, a safe and neutral individual who would not judge him for the shame, for being weak, for allowing Aaron to slash his innocence with selfish lust. He asks for referrals, makes a note of the names and telephone numbers, decides to throw away the list before placing even one call.

Instead of a therapist, he will tell a friend. He is ready now, ready to open the old envelope, admit it was not his mistake, it was not his fault, it was nothing more than someone taking advantage of an innocent boy. The confession will be a significant step toward his clean and sober future, a move toward wholeness, a safe place to discard the secret burning in his heart.

Riley smiles when I tell him I want to share a secret. We're in Santa Monica for a weekend retreat, avoiding our regular worlds, staying in a suite at the beach. These two- or three-day respites from reality have become a hallmark of our friendship. During the time that we both worked in New

York, Riley and I bonded over long lunches on the steps at Lincoln Center, recollecting our shattered childhoods, dissecting the dysfunction of our respective families. Now, a decade later in California, we return to the hotel after a lazy postlunch stroll, deciding to swim and nap in the late afternoon sunshine.

"Me too." He rolls onto his side, breaks the placid surface of the pool with his fingers. "I'm still starving."

"This isn't funny."

"Neither is malnutrition." Riley pulls his hand from the water, flicks a few random drops in my direction. "What do you want to tell me? What's the secret?"

I struggle to find the opening line, the beginning of the story. I start talking about the neighborhood in Kansas where I was raised, the ranch house and block parties and isolation I felt as an outsider in the picture-perfect suburban wasteland. I steer the story toward Aaron and his brother. I tell Riley that I was infatuated with the older boy, that I dreamed about him often, that I longed for his company, his attention, his praise.

Then I tell Riley about the afternoon alone with Aaron, the unfinished house, the embarrassment and agony of being raped by my best friend's brother. I am so consumed with the story that I'm no longer looking at Riley. My eyes are on the palm trees in the distance, the ruby blooms on the bougainvillea, our reflection in the sliding doors on the opposite side of the pool.

"Is that it?" Riley asks when my voice goes silent. "Is that the big, ugly secret?"

I nod. "Yep," I barely whisper. "That's the secret that I've been so afraid of for so many years."

Riley reaches over and rubs my neck. "It's done," he says. "That was over a long time ago. Just let it go. All of the old mistakes are gone now. Just let them go. They can't hurt you anymore. You're free now."

Riley's voice echoes softly in my mind. *All of the old mistakes are gone now.* Those eight words from my friend cannot erase the deeply etched grief from that childhood experience. Eight words cannot replace the decades of shame that began on that long-ago afternoon and radiated through my entire adult life. Eight words cannot remove the ripples of self-hatred that started with a despicable act of power and control and led to innumerable attempts on my part to exert power and control over my bedmates and lovers in the years that followed.

Eight words cannot quell my trembling spirit when I recall the pain from Aaron's attack. Eight words cannot unravel the tightly bound memories of grief. And Riley's eight words of advice alone cannot repair the damage from my drinking daze.

But they're a place to begin the healing, a mantra to remind myself that I am on my way. My ghosts may follow, but I will no longer allow them to lead. It is a new day.

15 / THE WORLD TURNED UPSIDE DOWN

Some love affairs last for an eternity, some for a brief moment before passion fails and the future is lost. In the failed affair with my liquid lover, there is suddenly no desire, no brilliant flame. There is no love, no deep and precious bond, nothing that demands I continue the relationship. I am free. I can fly alone. I'm ready to live again.

That's when the terror begins.

I have no idea what to do next. Therapy is an option. Joining a 12-step program is another. I could check myself into a clinic, disappear down a country lane and spend a month in a small motel with nothing but an ancient television and the drip, drip, drip of an antiquated faucet for companionship.

I could do many things to begin this new life. Change the locks on my front door. Exchange my telephone number for an unpublished seven digits to ensure privacy. I could reorganize my life, find a new job, discontinue my membership at Gold's Gym, move to an apartment in the suburbs.

I consider the options, knowing the entire time that I will do the one thing I should've done years ago to put myself on the path to healthy, happy living: I will turn my world upside down.

When I make the decision to regroup, restructure, revise, renew, and reorchestrate my life, I have no idea how long it will take before solidity and comfort replace tension, anxiety, grief, and remorse.

————

I walk down the aisle to find my seat on the flight to Newark. The plane is crowded, and I discover my seat is wedged between a pale young woman wearing lime-green overalls and a middle-aged man who looks like he's taking the first plane ride of his life.

"Are you going to New Jersey?" the man asks after I've securely fastened my seat belt. "This plane is going to Newark."

"Yes." I smile and open my *Vanity Fair*. "I'm going to Newark. I prefer to fly in and out of Newark when I visit friends in New York."

I start reading the horoscopes, trying to predict the month ahead using the inane text in a monthly zodiac listing. I sense that the man is staring, so I turn and smile.

"My wife was a Libra," he says. "She could never decide what direction to go or what to do next. Libras are so good at not making decisions."

I force a smile and make some blank statement about procrastination. The man says something about exceptions to every rule. I watch his lips move, but the only thing I can think is, *Terrific. As if I needed another reminder that I had trouble making choices. Is it too late to deplane?*

———

I realize early on that one commodity I gain along with sobriety is time. I have time to think, to plan, to dream. In the drinking days, I was always so busy running from today that I never planned or dreamed about tomorrow. There were occasional moments of clarity when I fantasized about the future. But those moments were easily washed away with an inch of Vitamin V poured over a bed of clear ice cubes.

Today time is no longer a threat; it is a blessing, a gift, a fragile entity to be tended and nurtured. I appreciate the beauty of each day and know that a new sunrise alone does not guarantee that life will be without ruts along the road.

In the early days of my sobriety, one of my greatest challenges is learning to make mistakes. Allowing myself to take a wrong turn, to feel sorrow and remorse and anger as everyday emotions of the human experience without using them as an excuse to overindulge in alcohol.

And still, even with years of sobriety and miles of happiness at my back, I get scared. Often.

I worry that I'll fail. Frequently.

I question my motives, the reasons I act or react, the sentences that escape my mouth when I'm fatigued or angry or lonely.

While these moments of dread and fear are just as real as they were during the drinking days, I am now capable of making rational, healthy decisions that lead to sane, balanced responses and choices.

When I'm the recipient of an unkind or dishonest remark, I have the confidence to correct the inaccuracy. I've also learned to let disharmonious moments roll away without leaving a mark or blemish on my heart. I forgive easily and often—the best way to repay the kindness I've received from friends, family, and strangers in my life.

I know I can't return to the drinking days and erase what was unkind or rebuild what was broken. I can, however, take special steps today to live my life with a smile on my lips, a prayer of compassion for all I meet, and an abundant passion for sharing goodness with others in order to send positive energy into the universe.

———

Riley wakes me up at 11 o'clock on my first day in New York to announce that we're going to Montauk. Considering that we'd been out dancing until 5 o'clock that morning, I'm less than thrilled with the thought of repacking my bag, jumping on the Jitney, and riding out to Long Island.

Riley's gorgeous face pouts better than anyone else's I know. I'm not surprised when his lower lip swells and he flops onto the bed when I protest his decision.

"Oh, c'mon," he says. "I want to go swimming in the ocean." In an instant, he's up off the bed, madly throwing T-shirts and beach towels and running shorts into a large canvas bag. "We'll be back tomorrow night in time for Nan's party."

I'm visiting Riley for the weekend. It's a few months after our Santa Monica siesta, and the objective for the trip was to help his sister celebrate her 30th birthday. Nan is a sweetheart, a dancer, a lunatic. When Riley told her I'd attempted suicide, she called immediately from a pay phone at JFK to berate me for an hour. "You will not do that again," she'd screamed, her voice drowning out the airline pages echoing in the background. "You are too intelligent to do something so stupid." I tried to explain that intelligence had nothing to do with my decision to leave the planet. She wouldn't listen.

Every word from my mouth only increased her volume, so I'd sat quietly and listened to her ramble and roar, knowing her fury was founded in love.

"If we go to Montauk, we'll miss the party," I tell Riley. He ignores me and continues packing. "Nan will be furious."

He tosses a paperback into the bag. "Nan's always furious," he says. "That's just her nature. Some people will always go for drama without thinking about how they seem to the rest of the world. Nan's one of those people."

That was me at one time, I think as I watch Riley change into a pair of clean khaki shorts and an Abercrombie T-shirt. *I don't ever want to be that disconnected again.*

———

Angels arrive when we need them, when we are ready for miracles, when we are ready for dreams to come true. Some angels are messengers; others are guardians and guides. In the first three years of my new life, I meet many angels. Each is a blessing, an aspect of the miracle, a thread in the rope that connects hope to humanity, truth to integrity, wisdom to the heart.

———

"Remember when you were drinking too much?" Riley asks. "Remember when it was cool to completely lose it?"

We're on the beach, watching the waves, listening to the wind.

"Why are we talking about this?"

"Just wondering," Riley says. "I went out and partied last week. It made me feel good. Then it made me feel bad."

Riley is struggling. On the drive to the beach, he tells me about his desire to remain sober. With three clean years under his belt, Riley wants to keep focused on his family, his career, the future. He knows that if he drinks, he will risk losing everything. Again.

Hearing him tell me that he relapsed a few days ago is killing me, but I remain calm and keep the conversation light.

"So you had a drink," I say. "That's OK. As long as you do it in moderation and work toward getting completely clean."

Riley is quiet. Then he says, "So, can you?"

"Can I what?"

"Can you remember when you were drinking too much? What's it feel like now? How's it different?"

————

He feels brave, courageous, terrified. This new world, this life without alcohol, is a dynamic dichotomy. It is neither heaven nor hell, hard nor soft, simple nor complex. It is a new place, filled with promise, fueled by purpose.

When he listens to the voices whispering from the past, whispering of indiscretions and infidelity and indecision, he fights the urge to erase himself from the landscape. He made mistakes. He stumbled. He fell and fought and failed to live a pure and unblemished life. He knows he cannot outrun the voices, that he will always hear whispers from long ago. He seeks gentle reminders in every day to reinforce the new direction of his sober life. He scans the horizon for proof he has been forgiven, although the one man who withholds permanent peace is himself. He knows forgiving himself will take time, and he must grasp every opportunity to remind himself that his addiction was behind the mistakes, the failures, the twists and turns of the drinking days.

He feels relief, knowing he made the only sane choice. He walked away from everything he knew and headed toward an unnamed destination on the far side of forever. He is walking still, one step at a time, toward his place on the planet. He has goals now, objectives and plans and dreams. Of course, he was always a dreamer, but the sober mind is capable of not only conjuring misty visions of hope and tomorrow; it can breathe life into dreams and make them sing and dance and move with light and love.

———

Back at the house, I lower the radio and turn to Riley. He's staring intently at the television, concentrating on the images that bounce through CNN's newscast like missiles of information and insight.

"It's like a complete reversal of fortunes," I say.

Riley looks at me. "What are you talking about?"

"Being sober," I say. "A few weeks ago, I was at a party and these women were completely wasted. I felt angry and sad all at the same time."

"Didn't you feel jealous?"

"Not at all. I just watched them and remembered when I was drinking. The difference between that time and today is like the world turned upside down."

"So you don't miss it?"

"I didn't say that. I just appreciate this new place much more. It feels good to wake up in the morning and remember what happened the night before. It feels good to make rational decisions. It feels good not to have constant rage and anger burning a hole in my heart."

Riley is quiet for a minute. "So you're glad you made the choice?"

"Every minute of every day," I tell him. "Every minute of every day."

16 / Faith & Blessings

I am alone in my truck, driving the concrete ribbon of highway that winds south through Chase County in eastern Kansas. The hills roll as far as I can see, dotted with livestock, trees, farmhouses. It's the winter of my second sober year, and I'm driving south for a weekend visit with my mother and sister. During the first few miles, I settle into the rhythm of the road. I love to drive. It gives me time to think and dream; time to map my course into the week ahead, the next month, the future.

There is uncertainty as I plan. As John Lennon wrote in a song to his son just months before his death, "Life is what happens when you're making other plans." Life rolls along, plans change, the road turns in an unexpected direction. The challenge is staying the course, maintaining a steady pace, moving forward.

I know how to do that now. I also know why I can do it. I have faith and I have blessings. Faith in myself, faith in my brothers, faith in a higher power. And the blessings? They're plentiful: an abundant and rich banquet of small favors and generous overtures, forgiveness from those I harmed or slighted, love from those I ignored or disdained.

It is not particularly fashionable for a gay man to speak of God. He is as politically incorrect as Republican politicians, straight fashion designers, or drag queens who do not worship Marilyn Monroe, Judy Garland, and Max Factor.

That's OK. I have my faith. Everyone else can have the higher power of his or her choice. For me, the gentle grace of an answered prayer surpasses all other experiences.

———

It's Christmas Eve, a chilly night without stars or wind. I'm sitting in a pew in a Presbyterian church between my mother and sister. My sister's family is with us: two daughters, a son, her husband of 20 years. As the congregation continues to arrive, I'm overcome by a feeling of sadness.

I'm 42 and there is no significant relationship in my life. I long for the comfort and familiarity of a love that runs deep, rather than the experiences I've had in the three years since I quit drinking. I want a deep emotional river to run through my heart and into another man's spirit.

"I feel strange," I whisper to my sister. "I remember what it was like when we were kids on Christmas Eve."

She leans toward me and speaks softly. "Good memories or bad?"

"Good." I fight the tears that threaten to run down my cheeks. "But I just feel so alone."

The congregation fills the church. The service begins. Candles glow in the dimly lit room. Music and song and celebration. I open the hymnal and begin to sing. It is the first time I've ever sung in church and I feel elated. I'm certain my voice is a random assault on the ears of those around me, but I don't care. I'm filled with a desire to join this chorus, to sing with these strangers in this room lit with candles and prayer and hope.

When I sit in the pew and listen to the lessons being read from the altar, my heart is calm and my mind is serene. I cannot attribute the unexpected change in my emotional state—from anxious and alone to calm and serene—to the simple act of singing in church for the first time, but I enjoy the thought. It has been years since I sought nourishment for my spiritual side, and I'm suddenly filled with the urgency to continue this new feeling by attending Sunday services when I return home after the holidays.

———

"This is good news," Quinn says when I call and tell him about my experience in church. "I hope you'll continue down that road. It's been a good choice for me."

Quinn is in his 10th year of sobriety, a decade of cleanliness after a lifetime of insanity and grief. We met in the early 1980s in San Francisco, a tired Tuesday night, a bar on Castro Street. I was in town on business, and Quinn was downing shots of whiskey and flipping a coin. Heads and he would stay in California. Tails and his tattered collection of paperbacks and party favors would cross the country to Boston. In the first few minutes of conversation, we discovered that we had both come of age in Kansas City. While I remained in the Midwest for years before moving to New York, Quinn followed his first love to the Bay Area. They lived for a year in Sausalito before the delicious first love gave Quinn a last good-bye kiss, leaving behind a broken heart and a bitter and confused young man. Quinn began drinking that night, the first entry in a long and wicked road that overflowed with sorrow, fear, loneliness, fatigue.

The friendship we began that Tuesday night in San Francisco continues to this day. We exchange stories about our drinking lives, uncovering similarities and coincidences that are simultaneously amusing and horrifying. To know that we've walked a similar path to our current clean place makes us brothers, comrades, survivors.

The development and nourishment of a safe circle of confidants is crucial to anyone in recovery. When I attended AA meetings, the participants frequently shared telephone numbers and insisted that it was appropriate to call at any time if the urge to drink became overpowering. I use my circle from time to time, when the shadows threaten and my strength loses its elasticity. It's easy to pick up the phone, dial the digits, share the fear and uncertainty.

"Did you ever think you'd be going to church on Sunday?" I ask Quinn. "Is it a strange change?"

He shakes his head. "I didn't think about it," he says. "It just happened. I was walking by a church in New York one weekend. I'd gone up early for a business meeting and decided to wander around and explore. I went to Central Park and headed down Fifth Avenue back to the hotel. I walked and walked and then stopped. I was right in front of a church. Before I thought about it, my feet just headed up the steps and inside."

Quinn describes the awakening he felt inside the sanctuary. It was a quiet, peaceful oasis, and he simply sat for an hour, thinking about the grace and beauty that had come into his life with the decision to quit drinking. He didn't kneel, didn't pray, didn't close his eyes in adulation. He just sat and reflected on the miracle of his sobriety and decided that it felt good to be in a church, thinking and studying and comparing the elements of his life.

"I guess it was another six months before I went back to church," Quinn tells me. "I had just started going out with

Brad. He belonged to a progressive Baptist church near my apartment. I know that's a contradiction, but it was a very cool community of open-minded people. I went with Brad one Sunday and then the next Sunday, and pretty soon it was something I did every week."

Talking with Quinn, I realize that the form is irrelevant, as is the location. In its most elementary fashion, spiritual growth and nourishment can happen anywhere at any time. I find it helpful to attend services at Unity Temple near my apartment. I read books written by Marianne Williamson, Melody Beattie, Anne Lamott. I consider their comments on faith, hope, and joy, and continue to build my own version of spirituality. It's like tailoring a garment that fits a body perfectly yet leaves room for necessary alterations in the future.

"I remember Sundays from when I was drinking," Quinn says. "I'd wake up somewhere between noon and hell. My head would echo with every sound, and I'd usually vomit a time or two before I could move into the living room."

"Very attractive," I interject. "Nothing I'd know about."

"Uh-huh. You know *exactly* what I'm talking about. The only thing my spirit got in those days was a momentary reprieve from punishment. I'd be too hungover to do anything truly destructive. One or two drinks in the early evening would put me in bed by 10. And church? I don't think so."

As Quinn rambles on with his story, I start thinking about my spirit. It is healthy, invigorated, active, and alive. It breathes with life, burns with determination, and extends a loving hand whenever needed. The difference between the drinking days and the present time is a miracle, a blessing. I know I will maintain this course and continue to feed and cleanse my ethereal side so it can provide the direction and determination for my new life.

"You tired of talking about this?" Quinn asks when he pauses. "Or should we go on?"

"Let's go on," I say. "I want to continue this dialogue for the rest of my life."

Quinn's laugh fills the phone. "OK," he says. "Sometimes when we talk like this, I can't believe it's us. It's so far from where we used to be."

Now it's my turn to laugh. "That's right," I tell Quinn. "That's because we are far away from who we used to be. We're new men, and we've got a great second chance at life."

And we do. This new life is a miracle, a blessing, a gift, and I intend to cherish its true and simple beauty with the dawn of each new day.

17 / HOPE

Survivors talk of miracles, angels, luck. The man who changes his airline reservation on a whim, missing a plane that plummets to earth on a stormy night. A child who escapes death by turning left instead of right moments before the ceiling collapses in a shopping mall. An addict in Denver who sits outside of his dealer's house in Aurora, searching for the missing bills he needs to buy another gram of Peruvian powder, narrowly avoiding a shower of bullets.

It is easy to listen to other survivors describe the beauty and sanctity of their new lives and instantly recognize the moments of grace and hope that begin to define the progress drinkers make when they choose a sober life. It is more difficult to distinguish those moments in my own life. The static that bleeds into the day distorts my view; after a few months, I wish my new outlook came with a warning decal in the lower right corner of every glance: "Objects in your path may appear larger than in real life."

But this is real life. And the objects do appear larger, more foreboding and dangerous, until I learn to appraise each day with care and precision. In the drinking days, decisions flowed like water from a defective tap; a ceaseless stream of verdicts and choices based not on fact, reason and logic but on an unpredictable pattern of irrational and selfish behavior.

Today, when someone returns to the scene of a past indiscretion, recounting how horribly I behaved at one moment in the past or the cavalier and insensitive attitude I displayed, I want to say one thing to them: *So shoot me. I was a drunk. I'm better now.*

And I am better now. I have hope. I have clarity. And I have purpose. My life has evolved from a collection of random and occasionally idiotic moves into a gorgeously choreographed plan. At one time, I stumbled and hesitated, an awkward and embarrassed misfit. Today, I leap and soar, a confident man moving with patience and faith through the ups and downs of everyday life without resorting to an escape clause or flight plan the moment I become uncomfortable or angry or tired or lonely.

Life is good.

There is hope.

And there is a future.

When people ask me about my romance with liquor, about the affair and its effect on my life, they ask if I have regrets and misgivings. I tell them I have residual guilt about certain events, actions, words, and deeds from the drinking days. I also tell them I have accepted those aspects of the drinking years as a part of the plan, a portion of the journey I was destined to take.

If the same people ask about shame and guilt and innocence today, if I can handle the difference between my drinking life and the way I live, I always answer with confidence and thankfulness.

Yes, I tell them. I can handle it all because I have the one thing I never had during the dark days. I have the one element that makes everything possible, the bridge that helped me make the journey between the old life and this new, blessed place.

I have hope.

———

I am sitting in the lobby of a hotel in Honolulu, watching the curtain of rain that obscures the view of the beach. I am drinking my sixth cup of McDonald's coffee, smoking another Marlboro, wishing the day had started with a sunrise instead of a gray wall of water. In my room upstairs, waiting for dawn, I have already consumed a pair of books, several magazines, a carton of wheat crackers, and bottled water. Around five o'clock, I decide to start drinking coffee. I am waiting for my friend to fly in from Portland, wondering when the sky will clear, wishing I'd packed a certain cassette tape with selected Joan Armatrading tracks. Her music has always evoked thoughts of hope and harmony, the soundtrack for salvation and rebirth.

"This is a good day?"

The woman is thin and short, a tiny wisp of life dressed in peach walking shorts, a dark blue windbreaker, and a baseball cap. She looks to be in her 60s, a seasoned veteran of the sudden rain showers that sweep through Hawaii with regularity throughout the day at this time of year.

"Yes." I blot the cigarette into the ashtray. "I hope it will be a good day."

She motions to the seat beside mine. When I nod and smile, she sits back into the palm tree–patterned cushions and crosses her legs. She looks like a doll, a tiny creature swallowed by enormous hotel furniture.

"I am here for vacation." She pulls a small billfold from her pocket, unsnapping the closure with a soft click. "My husband would come with me, but he is sick." She opens the billfold and holds it up so I can see a photograph. In the picture, the woman is standing beside a man in a wheelchair. They are smiling at the camera, twin statements of happiness and love.

"Is he at home, then?"

She tells me he is back in Oakland. She describes his most recent round of surgery, something minor related to his heart condition. Then she tells me that their son and daughter are caring for their father.

"I wanted to stay with him," she says, "but we always come to the islands this time of year. Thirty-six years and we always spend our anniversary in Hawaii."

She turns and looks through the window at the rain. A few pedestrians walk quickly down the street, trying to stay dry beneath their umbrellas and rain hats. The woman closes the billfold, another soft click, and slips it back into her pocket.

"He's probably very happy that you made the trip," I tell her, not knowing what else to say. "You'll be able to go back home with stories for him so that he'll be ready to come next year."

It is natural to talk about the future. This stranger in a hotel lobby on a rainy morning in May is familiar with hope, comfortable with compassion, connected to the possibility that tomorrow will be brighter than today. In just a few minutes, she's described details from her life that tell me she's resilient and brave: the wheelchair, the heart surgery, the solo journey to this paradise for lovers.

"It's doubtful that we'll come back together," she says. "The doctors are not hopeful about his condition." She takes a breath, squeezes her hands into miniature fists. "But I tell him everything I see and the places I go, and it will be alive again for him, even if it's just for a short time. That's how we share our love. That's what gives him hope."

———

Cleaning my bureau drawers one morning, I find a post-card from Christian, sent three years ago, sealed in an envelope from the Peninsula Hotel in Los Angeles: "Why do you try to explain yourself? I have never felt more intense sadness or more silliness than with you. I am looking at your picture...the one from Loose Park. It is gorgeous. You are deadly. I surrender."

Reading the note, I try to connect the dots that brought Christian into my life. It began after a lunch at Houston's with Riley and his friends from New York. They were driving to Los Angeles, four adventurers in one rental car with a common dislike of air travel and an uncommon disregard for schedules and calendars. I met them at the restaurant near my apartment. It was a raucous meal; bad Drew Barrymore gossip and grilled chicken and boys being boys.

After lunch we walked through Loose Park. Riley photographed everyone in the Rose Garden; individual poses, group shots, two complete rolls of film. I never saw the pictures and nearly forgot the time in the park until the note arrived from Christian.

Christian is Riley's friend from college, a pleasant and polite man with perfect teeth, a pristine complexion, and a polite disposition. He holds the door for strangers, offers his smile freely, flirts with men and women like no one I've ever met. The day we strolled through the park, Christian and I talked about movies and music and friendship and the consequences of a life lived without hope. He told me that his mother had been in rehab three times before she ended her struggle with a single bullet from his father's hunting rifle.

When he told me about his mother's suicide, I watched Christian's face. It was calm and flat, no visible signs of distress or sorrow. He shifted from telling about his mother to a funny vignette from his childhood, a long story about how he learned Santa Claus wasn't real.

I've had many conversations with new faces during the past three years, looking for fresh lessons, offering words of support and succor, enjoying the commerce of two minds engaged in verbal discourse. They have all been helpful on some level, but the time I spent talking to Christian in the park seemed to have had a concrete and lasting impact on him.

Even as I read his note again after I discover it beneath a pile of boxer shorts, it feels both unusual and uncomfortable. After living as a paper-thin man for so many years, trying to travel undetected through my own life, it feels strange to hear that I caused an emotional reaction in someone I spent a few hours with in a park on a Saturday afternoon.

It takes several months, but I soon learn that these connections will provide sustenance and growth to my sobriety. I will derive strength and faith from unexpected encounters, random dialogues of words and fragments and comments knit together into conversation. I will also learn that these connections are a major part of my recovery, allowing me to share my story with others who struggle to quit drinking.

I read Christian's note again, bury the postcard back in my bureau drawer, search for his address in my journal. Later that day, I buy a blank card and write a reply to his question: "Why do I try to explain myself? Because I must. It helps me to understand, to learn, to grow. Sobriety may begin with a choice, the decision not to drink, but it grows with each passing day like a rose until it bursts forth with a beautiful bloom of faith, integrity, and honor. Love, John."

————

One afternoon not long after I celebrate my sixth sober month, I'm sitting in Starbucks in Santa Monica with Riley.

His schedule is clear for a few days, and he's invited me to California for a long weekend of rest. Over the years, Santa Monica has become one of our favorite places to meet for a respite from life, work, addiction.

"Now what?" Riley asks. "What's your next move?"

"My next move with what?"

He glares at me through the steam that levitates above his latte. "You know what I mean. How are you going to stay sober? How will you get started?"

I go for the easy laugh. "By not drinking vodka," I say. "That sounds like a good place to start."

Riley shakes his head, pinches his nose. "That stinks. What are you *really* going to do next?"

I've been thinking about the same question for the past few weeks. The time in Hawaii gave me a chance to refocus my energy and interests, to create a few realistic goals. I would make slow, deliberate choices about how I spend my time, who I see in social situations, where I go for pleasure. I would study my past and identify the factors that trigger my drinking. Some would be obvious: sorrow about the end of my friendship with Dylan; shame about the things I did and said during my final four-day binge; the insecurity that has gnawed at my spirit throughout my life; the anxiety that occasionally turns my private mumbling into concrete monsters that stumble during the most basic public situations.

I share these thoughts with Riley. He sits quietly and listens as I ramble and roam across the past few years. He's heard me describe my fears and phobias before, so the summary I deliver is familiar to him. When I start to dig deeper— to talk about how I've always felt like an outsider, a loner, a failure—Riley sits up in his chair and asks me to stop.

"I had no idea you felt that way," he says. "Why didn't you tell me about this before?"

I consider his question for a moment. "I didn't tell you," I say, "because I couldn't tell myself. I couldn't face the truth.

I was too busy trying to make myself fit into the world to worry about the reasons I felt like a misfit."

"So it was about pride?"

I look at Riley. "I'd say it was more about fear. I was so afraid people wouldn't like who I was that I drenched myself in alcohol."

Riley reaches across the table, grabs my hand. "We're all afraid at one point or another," he says. "Just know now that I'm here when you get frightened. I'm here, and Beth and your other friends. We've been here the whole time. Now maybe you can reach out and let us know when you're afraid. OK?"

I know the answer. And I feel blessed to have my friends. I know that their support will be essential to my survival. After a few minutes, I squeeze Riley's hand and say, "Thank you. I'm lucky to know you."

Riley laughs. "No," he says. "We're lucky to know each other. That's how this friendship thing works. Don't ever be afraid again to tell me anything. That's the deal. That's how it goes from here on out. OK?"

I answer with another smile, lean my face back into the sunshine, and bathe in the beauty of the golden day and my good fortune.

———

He does not want to be considered weak. Incomplete. Ruled by a substance. Overpowered by a drug. He wants to be seen as sensible and courteous and responsible. He wants to be known as friendly, gregarious, thoughtful. The kind of guy who receives a constant stream of social invitations from a wide circle of friends. Dinner parties and Cinco de Mayo fiestas and gallery openings and graduation celebrations and poolside gatherings where everyone is seen as sensible and courteous and responsible.

He murmurs the same mantra to himself when he feels frightened: *It's fine. You're going to be OK. Don't worry about what they think. Forget what they say. It's OK. You're going to be fine.*

The words tumble and blur and blend into a blanket that provides a home for his rattled heart.

Why do they say he's weak? So many reasons to overindulge. A bad relationship. The unexpected tax audit. Words of rejection from a coworker. The death of a close friend. Feelings of inferiority, the compulsive buzz that generates when the message that ripples into his mind, across his heart, is the same numbing signal day after day after day.

The message that he is weak and incomplete because he is ruled by a substance and overpowered by a drug. The message that mixes with another signal, a broadcast from deep within his spirit, the mantra that is telegraphed continually to instill some sense of peace and pride until the moment when he escapes the poison and finds a way to walk free.

It's fine. You're going to be OK. Don't worry about what they think. Forget what they say. It's OK. You're going to be fine.

———

Paul and I are walking along the waterway that winds through the Country Club Plaza near my apartment. It is a Tuesday evening in July, uncharacteristically cool for a summer night, and we are strolling and talking after dinner at Eden Alley. Paul is visiting Kansas City from New York. He has come to town to teach a five-week series of technique classes for a local ballet troupe.

As we walk, he looks overhead and smiles. "In Copenhagen," he says, "this time of day is called the blue hour."

I glance across the boulevard, over the water and up into the heavens. The sky is a pale azure plane, a beautiful blue surface that arcs over our heads and glows at its most distant limits in the west and east.

"What took you to Copenhagen?" I ask, trying to learn as much as I can about Paul during the brief time we spend together during the final week of his stay in Kansas City. "How long did you live there?"

Paul tells me he moved to Denmark when the end of his career as a ballet dancer in New York dovetailed with the beginning of his love affair with a Danish man. "It was a wonderful time in my life," Paul says. "But now I'm glad to be back in America, living where I don't have to always think, 'I wonder what they *really* meant by that comment.' "

As Paul continues to talk about his three years in Copenhagen, I hold his comment about the trepidation associated with translation. I imagine his experience and realize that his life as an American expatriate living in Denmark is similar to my experiences as a sober man living in Gay America.

The concept of translation and interpretation was a constant theme when I was drinking. I was always on guard about the true meaning of someone's comments, actions, or intentions. The slow hiss of paranoia filtered through conversations and messages left on answering machines and notes sent through the mail.

In the years I am writing about, I could not trust anyone because I could not trust myself. There was no certainty or conviction in my motives and actions. Instead, a reckless series of random events, overheard remarks, and statements lifted out of context embroidered the dispirited proof that I was a man without hope, without trust, without faith.

As I walk along the water, listening to Paul describe the sensation of returning to America after three years in a foreign land, I am amazed at the similarities between his experiences and my life as a sober man. Without a waterfall of alcohol to distort the shape and meaning of symbols, language, emotions, I can see everything clearly.

"It must be amazing," Paul says. "To have this experience of being sober."

"It's a miracle," I say. "A small miracle in the grand scheme of things, but a miracle to me. I never thought I could live like this, never dreamed it would happen. But it has. And I'm grateful every day. This clarity gives me hope that all things are possible, and if I can share the hope with other men, I will be returning the love given to me when I was at the bottom."

Paul smiles, reaches over, and rests his hand on my shoulder. "You're going to be a good friend to many people," he says. "I can tell that right now."

Later that night, alone in my bed, I remember Paul's remark and I know he's right. I will be a good friend to others in need, because I've finally learned to be a good friend to myself.

18 / SLOW

In conversations with other men who survive addiction, the subject of boundaries is frequent and familiar. While our past may be littered with endless examples of the lack of boundaries, we must learn to define, establish, and enforce emotional, sexual, and psychological limits that are appropriate, healthy, and meaningful.

On paper, setting boundaries is a simple premise. The cause and effect between how someone treats me and how I respond is defined in specific, pristine images. It's not as if I walk around with a small guidebook tucked in my trouser pocket, a code of conduct I can consult when a situation appears to be headed for a difficult moment.

Each day is filled with the opportunity to question motives, relationships, and results. Is this healthy behavior? Am I acting responsibly? Will the outcome of this experience be beneficial? Do I want to date this man? Should I sleep with this guy? Am I dating *this* man and sleeping with *that* guy because I fear my behavior is unhealthy and I'm acting irresponsibly?

For the first few sober months, I spend every day like a psychotic juggler. I question motives and calculate outcomes and attempt to second-guess every possible variable.

In the end, I'm exhausted. And frustrated. And tense. It's only during a phone call with Kathryn, a childhood friend who now pursues her cinematic dreams in California, that I realize the key to setting boundaries is to proceed at a slow pace.

There is something unnatural about this decision. It is awkward and aberrant, a complete deviation from the patterns and currents of my life. During the final four years of the drinking days, I became increasingly impatient. And irritated. And irrational. The premise that I would pace myself through the decisions and choices and experiences of a normal day is absurd, a concept sliced from someone else's life and grafted onto my own.

Wait to make a rational choice? Consider the consequences of my action before I act? Weigh the outcome and delay my own pleasure and satisfaction? No. No, thank you very much, but I want what I want when I want it. If not sooner.

———

There is an unappetizing swagger invoked when some men speak openly about recovery. As if they are somehow designated holier than those who remain entrenched in the disease. As if they are better than their brothers who wake with heavy heads and foggy regrets, who crawl from one heartache to the next because they have not yet reached the bottom of their bruised experience with alcohol. As if they rise higher on the food chain when they succeed at sobriety.

As if.

Whether these sober men can find the strength to admit it or not, we are all in this together. We are divided by choices, slogans, designations. Top and bottom, fem and butch, daddy and boy, lover and loved, trick and treat, and rock and roll.

———

Ron is a graphic artist and avid runner who now spends his weekends training for marathons instead of racing from one Long Island iced tea to the next. He's lean and relaxed when we meet for a late afternoon lunch at McCoy's Pubhouse in Westport. It's been a few weeks since our last conversation, and Ron launches into an animated monologue about his next long-distance race even before the waiter takes our beverage order.

"It's going great," Ron tells me. "I've never felt this focused before. I think it'll be my best time yet."

"Do you remember running when you were still drinking?"

He looks up and beams me with his smile. "That was more like crawling," he says. "I used to force myself out for a run the day after getting smashed. God, it was insane. I'd struggle through my course and then collapse. My heart would feel like it was going to explode in my chest. I always finished, though. I thought if I kept to my workout schedule, I'd somehow make up for the night before."

Ron and I met at Loose Park one Sunday afternoon about six months before I quit. He was three years sober at that point, although the subject of sobriety didn't enter our conversations until a year or so after I went dry.

He was obviously a serious runner, and I was a weekend wanna-be. I too was straining to maintain a fitness regimen, despite my constant diet of Vitamin V and wine. That Sunday afternoon in October, Ron was stretching beside his car when I pulled into the parking lot and began to warm up for my three-mile run. He looked familiar, and it wasn't until a few minutes into our conversation that I recognized him from the dance floor at the Cabaret.

It had been a couple of years since I was out dancing, but I remembered Ron's face: bee-stung lips, eyes that are set wide apart, and a mile-deep dimple in his chin. He's not drop-dead gorgeous, but there's a vibrancy that glows from his gaze, and I must have picked up on that at the Cabaret, even though I was probably a wreck when I saw him. Funny how some memories survive the alcoholic assault and others perish.

———

A month into my first year of sobriety, I'm at a bookstore near my apartment, flipping through a new novel in the fiction section, when I hear a familiar voice.

"Hey, stranger. Is this where you've been hiding?"

It's Jack, a familiar face from the past, a man who was as much of a fixture on the bar circuit as I was during the drinking days. Jack and I used to sit at the bar near the pool tables at the Cabaret, smoking cigarettes and drinking while we waited for someone appetizing to appear.

"So?" Jack stands in the aisle, one hand on the bookshelf, the other hand on his hip. He's aging fast; the hair on his temples is now fully gray, and the lines around his eyes are deeper and more defined than I remember.

"So what?" I smile and try to deflect his stern gaze. "I've been around."

"You haven't been around where I've been around," Jack says. "What's going on? I ran into Phillip at the White Party and he said he hadn't seen you in months."

"That's probably true. I think the last time I saw Phillip was at the DB. Maybe the Other Side. I can't remember."

Jack's head flips to the right as a handsome man walks past. Perpetually on the prowl and allegedly interested in a relationship, Jack is the kind of man who enjoys shopping for a boyfriend more than making the purchase.

"You look pretty good," Jack says. "Anyone new in your life?"

"Not really. I've been busy with work."

I can tell from the way he screws his mouth into a tight smirk that he doesn't buy my answer. I can also tell from the foggy look in his eyes and the dryness of his skin that Jack's probably just as active today as he was when I used to match him drink for drink at the Cabaret.

"What's really going on?" he says. "I worried that maybe you'd moved or something, but Phillip said you were still in the same apartment. Are you OK?"

Jack's eyes tell me that he's referring not to my fiscal or mental health but to my HIV status.

"I'm doing great," I tell him. "My health couldn't be better." I look at the book in my hands and return it to the shelf. Then I say, "Actually, something has changed. I quit drinking. I don't go out much anymore. That's why you haven't seen me around."

For a minute, I feel a ripple of embarrassment ride across my face, like telling the truth will somehow wound Jack's sensitive heart. I've felt this several times in the past year, thinking I will somehow offend the men who continue to drink heavily when I mention the story of my recovery. As I listen to Jack talking about a new John Grisham book he's reading, I realize that I need to share my story with him. I need to let him know why I've dropped out of the social circus we once shared, how glorious it is to be clean, how sobriety has elevated my life to a new level of clarity and purpose.

"Do you have time for coffee?" I ask when Jack finishes. "I want to tell you something."

———

There is always a reason to justify a blackout or a binge, always an explanation for another weekend lost to liquor and dancing and sex with a stranger. There is always an excuse, a believable tale to tell anyone who questions the events of the previous evening.

"Oh, my God," he says when someone tries to learn why he disappeared for two days. "I met the most amazing guy."

"And that's why you couldn't return my call?"

"We clicked, like, instantly. It was so bizarre. Wait until you meet him!"

"That's great. I'd still like an explanation. Why didn't you show up at the benefit? We held that place at the table for you because you said you'd be there. And then you didn't even bother to call? What's going on with you?"

What's going on is gradual erosion. One grain of sand at a time dissolves and disappears, threatening the foundation, endangering the future. At this stage, when obligations are ignored and friendships begin to suffer and the common responsibilities of a sane life are disregarded, there is no concept of going slow. The train is plummeting down a steep incline, and the center will not hold.

"Trust me," he says. "I'm fine. I just met this amazing guy and he swept me off my feet." A smile and a nod seal the lie with the words that become a drinker's mantra, the phrase that is repeated most often in the betrayal of heart, mind, and spirit. "I'm sorry."

The true tragedy is that he says he is sorry, but he's incapable of making the connection between the words and the responsibility required to say them with honesty and sincerity.

"I'm sorry," he says again as he eyes the exit and plots his escape. "I'm really sorry."

And he is.

Really sorry. He is miserable and sad, a woeful man with a wretched outlook and a deplorable attitude and the inability to realize that the word *sorry* in this situation applies not to *how he feels* but to *who he is*.

19 / INVENTING HAPPINESS

Matt arrives wearing faded 501s and a black polo, with a cell phone glued to his left ear. I close the door and go into the kitchen to cook while he finishes the conversation. I overhear a few comments; mostly talk of his children, their swimming lessons, an extra-credit summer school project for his son.

When he finishes the call, Matt finds me in the kitchen.

"I'm sorry." His arms encircle me like a marble trap, strong and steady and cold. "I couldn't get Christina off the phone."

I tell him it's not a problem. He tells me about his son's accomplishments at camp. I listen and stir the pasta and check the chicken breasts in the oven. I am cooking dinner again for the first time in years, walking the culinary tightrope with a spatula in one hand and *Joy of Cooking* in the other. Dylan and I cooked in this kitchen nearly every night of the week, and it's taken more than two years to prepare a meal for another man in this space. It feels like being a widow returning to the dance floor with another partner.

"And so I told him that he was courageous and wise," Matt is saying. "Do you think that was the right thing to do?"

"You always do the right thing," I say, wondering what we're talking about.

I can't concentrate on Matt's story, because I'm doing what I promised myself I wouldn't do: straddling the divide between the past and the present. I'm cooking rigatoni and chicken breasts for this evening's meal, yet my mind is overflowing with images of Dylan in this same room. Dylan washing the dishes. Dylan cooking omelets. Dylan mixing our morning protein shakes. He was always clumsy in the kitchen, spilling and dropping and burning. But that was part of his charm.

"No, I don't." Matt snaps a towel at my rear. "You're just being polite. I can screw up sometimes, too. We all can."

I know he's talking about his son and the summer camp, but I'm trying to focus on the present moment. I want to be honest with Matt and give him the attention he deserves. In the months since we met, he's filled my life with friendship and unconditional love. The pieces are falling into place and it's no longer necessary to invent happiness; it's happening around me every day of the week. And even though it is a strange sensation, I want to stay in this place for a very long time.

———

He is happy, favored by fortune, pleased with his life. The state of being content and cheerful is foreign, and he realizes that comfort with happiness will come with time. He smiles, he laughs, and he finally finds the connection between expressing happiness and living it.

He has, after many years of searching, finally reached home.

––––

"Listen," Matt says later. "Can we talk?"

"About?"

He wants to talk about his brother, Erik. We're leaving for the airport in an hour to meet Erik's flight from Salt Lake City. Erik has been living in Utah for three years, working for a bank, wrestling with the guilt he feels about his divorce. When Matt told me Erik was leaving his wife, I suspected it was the result of drink. In college, before he married and moved west, Erik and I were lovers for a few months. Matt had introduced us after a tennis match. "This is my little brother," he'd said. "Don't corrupt him." A few weeks later, when I ran into Erik at the Cabaret, it was his idea to leave the bar and finish the evening with cocktails and passion at his parents' house.

Erik and I drank a lot that summer. We also slept together on a regular basis. Although he claimed to be struggling with his true orientation, I felt an aggressive urgency in his kiss and the touch of his hand. I wasn't surprised when Matt told me about Erik's engagement to Alicia. And I wasn't surprised that I didn't receive an invitation to the wedding. But I was astonished when I heard that Erik was drinking heavily and beating his new wife within six weeks of the wedding. Fear and denial can be postponed, but they cannot be vanquished by drink. I comforted Matt a few times with lengthy conversations, trying to help him realize that he couldn't control Erik's behavior.

I agree to accompany Matt to the airport. I want to see Erik. I want him to know that I care. And I want him to know that he's safe with me; a secure harbor is crucial to an alcoholic who is fully engaged in battle. I want Erik to know that he can count on me to help, if he chooses to ask for it.

"Something is going on with him," Matt says. "I've been getting these weird calls. He doesn't always make sense. It's like he starts a story and gets sidetracked before he finishes one thought."

I tell Matt I know about those calls. There was a time when I made them to many friends and family members, the drunken, senseless ramble, a desperate attempt to reach out to shore when I was drifting into turbulent waters.

"It'll be OK," I say. "Let's see how he's doing when his plane lands. Maybe he'll be in a great mood and we'll have a chance to talk."

———

Find me. I will wait. Capture my heart. I will capture yours. Take this moment to tell me one secret. Breathe this life into your soul. Angels come when we are ready.

Find me.

———

Everybody knows. OK, everybody knows except me. For years I struggle to avoid the obvious, and I am the last to know: Happiness is a journey, not a destination. For years and years and years, for *decades,* I appeared to be happy. On the surface there was a smile, a pair of gleaming eyes, a beaming, bright light of contentment and joy.

When your universe is defined by drink and denial, deception is easy. With one word, one sentence, one kiss on the cheek, I was able to project the appearance of sobriety or moderation. I hate the memories that crowd my mind like a forest of infidelity and grief. Memories of telling friends and boyfriends that I was doing fine as I was getting ready to rendezvous with my lover at a nearby liquor store, party, bar, or restaurant.

Breaking the cycle of deception is difficult. I still find myself lurching toward a lie rather than leaning toward the truth. The programming in my mind is incomplete. It combines old tapes from the drinking daze and new information from the years of clean and sober living. Despite my best efforts, the two occasionally intersect and cause a short circuit in my brain. In response to a simple question, I feel a fabrication forming on my lips. I struggle to keep the lie contained in order to develop an honest response to the question.

I don't want to lie, but old habits are hard to break. I know I must be patient with myself. It may take years before the old tapes are completely replaced by new, healthy material. In the meantime, I'll keep a watchful eye on myself.

———

"If you know yourself well enough," Matt says with the solemnity of a Sunday sermon, "you know when you're truly happy."

We're sitting in traffic on Broadway, waiting for the red light to blink over to green. Even with the air conditioning and the iced cappuccino, I feel like I'm melting into the black leather seats of Matt's car.

"Do you feel happy?" Matt asks.

I tell him that I feel moist. "It's too hot to have a serious conversation," I say. "Can we just ride in silence for a few miles?"

"No," Matt shouts, increasing the car's speed and the radio's volume simultaneously, "I want to know what's going on with you. Are you happy?"

"Yes," I say, leaning over so he can hear me above the Hendrix solo. "I feel very, very happy."

I ease back in the seat, look at my reflection in the rear view mirror, and whisper, "At last."

———

It is a difficult point to admit. I am happy. After years of indoctrination in my parents' house—where I was schooled in the art of blank expression, stoicism, and frozen hearts—I didn't discover the amazing freedom of self-love and self-expression until I was in my 40th year.

I'm happy. I'm content. I will be honest and direct, even if it proves to be an expensive action in the marketplace of romance and companionship. If I don't feel like going to dinner after I agree to make plans, I will cancel. If I fail to return a phone call within a 24-hour period, I will no longer feel guilt or remorse. I will remember to forgive myself at these moments.

———

Matt parks at the curb outside the TWA gates at the airport. He tells me to wait while he runs inside to find his brother. I lower the window and feel the wave of hot, dry air. It's like a cashmere blanket, warm and luxurious and sensuous. I put my head back and close my eyes, thinking about the writing project I'm finishing for a client.

"Plane's here, but Erik isn't."

I open my eyes and look up at Matt. The tension in his jaw and the wide rage of his eyes tells me there's trouble. "Something wrong?"

"He missed the flight."

Matt climbs behind the wheel, starts the car and spins angrily into traffic. I brace myself against the seat and wait a few minutes before I say anything. When we're back on the highway and his breathing has returned to normal, I suggest we stop for coffee and dessert. At Starbucks, Matt grips the counter with the ferocity of a gladiator colliding with his opponent.

"What happened?" I ask. "Is he OK?"

Matt's nostrils flare, his grip tightens on the menu. When he speaks, his voice is a volcanic flow, hot and deadly and unforgiving. "I'm done with him. He's fucked up too many times."

Matt turns and stares into the distance. I watch his face, the corners of his mouth, the tremor beneath his skin as he clenches his teeth. I watch him and wonder how many times people have said that same sentence about me.

———

He is learning how to be patient. As a young boy, he was taught that patience is a virtue. The lesson was meaningless, because no one taught him the definition of virtue. Throughout his life, the concept was incomplete. He knew it was a good thing to be patient, but he never knew why. He knew he should wait. He knew he shouldn't speak until someone addressed him first. And he knew he should sit quietly in his chair until his parents had finished eating dinner.

Being patient was just one of the concepts he failed to understand as he made the transition between youth and adulthood. He was also confused about self-worth, individual identity, his role in the greater community known as humanity. Within the walls of his father's house, he could bargain for acceptance and the chilly connection his parents employed in lieu of unconditional love. He learned he would be rewarded with his favorite things—a new bike, a bowl of ice cream, a less harsh spanking—if he maintained a passive presence.

As time passed, the quiet, flaccid exterior enveloped him. He felt uncomfortable in crowds. He worried he would be ridiculed if he spoke his true opinion. He felt alone, forgotten, disconnected.

Until he met his liquid lover.

With the hot power of alcohol pumping through his spirit, he learned to feel at ease in a crowd. After one or two drinks, he spoke openly and cared little for the opinions of others. He felt larger than life, important, at peace.

Until alcohol betrayed him on a peaceful Sunday afternoon in April and he floundered in an ocean of agony. He succumbed to the waves of terror and pain that had been kept away for so long by the constant drip, drip, drip of his liquid lover's kiss.

It would take years of quiet patience to finally embrace happiness and find that the light of his own smile was enough of an ember to let him walk forward into the unknown territory of each new tomorrow.

———

Matt sits in the brown velour chair in the back of Starbucks. He's staring over his left shoulder, through the glass window wall, transfixed by a swirl of cocoa-colored leaves that sweep along the empty brick walkway. He hasn't said a word in 20 minutes, and I'm waiting for the anger to burn off before I venture into verbal territory.

The time with Matt has been a good lesson for me. One of the most essential elements of my sobriety today is remembering yesterday. The rage that ignited in Matt's mind and roared through his voice at the airport reminds me of anger I've experienced before. It also reminds me that I've learned the serenity and joy of patience with myself and others, one of the most important lessons of this new life.

20 / BELIEVE

In my third year of sobriety, I begin to realize that it's less important to measure my progress than it is to live a progressive life. There is concrete proof that I'm better. There is the fluidity of my speech, optimistic behavior, the improved financial infrastructure, a new job, a new romance after many false starts.

As I write this sentence, I have been alcohol-free for nearly 1,000 days. In the frenetic scramble of everyday life, I sometimes forget the brilliance and beauty of that simple fact.

I am sober. I am sane. And I am happy. For alcoholics, *sober, sane,* and *happy* are elusive goals that fade and flicker in the distance while we're busy running from whatever it is that scared us in the first place.

And when we stop running? Only then do we have a chance to heal, to better our hearts and minds so we can experience every aspect of life. I remember the first few months of sobriety. As my heart healed and my mind awoke, the simple pleasures and textures and tastes of everyday life were explosive and unimaginably exciting. Rebuilding my routine was beyond rewarding; it seemed mystical that I could carry myself through a 24-hour period and accomplish mundane tasks—making my bed, washing the dishes, returning telephone calls from friends and family members—as well as the more elevated aspirations of my newfound spirit—sharing love and support with those in need and finding a place in each day to give thanks for my return to the land of the living.

Small miracles are wondrous moments of unexplained beauty and unparalleled grace. For years I dreamed about a miracle happening in my life: the miracle of sobriety. Now that it's become reality, I know that miracles happen on a daily basis. We'll know them only if we keep our eyes open and hearts receptive.

———

"I thought I would die the moment Jason left me," Harrison says. "I thought my world was collapsing around me. But I was wrong. Life goes on. It's just taken me a while to go along with life."

Harrison stands in the center of the room, weaving an intricate knot of fingers and knuckles and tension as he tells our small group about his life. He was raised by an abusive mother and an alcoholic father. When he was an undergrad at the University of Kansas, studying business and economics, Harrison fell in love with a man from Iowa named Jason. They spent a dozen years together, and Harrison struggled with his drinking the entire time. In the end, Jason packed his bags one night and announced that he was leaving.

"He told me he loved me when I was sober," Harrison

tells the group. "But he hated me when I was drunk."

As Harrison pauses to sip from a glass of water, I begin to think about the parallels between our lives. His Jason was my Dylan. His denial was my denial. And his heartbreak was my agony. Only now, three years down the road to clean and sober, can I listen to a story that echoes my own and realize that I've come a long way. I've made progress, gained new insight and wisdom. I'm better. And the key to staying better is to remember the past without reliving it, to embrace the present without suffocating it, and to envision the future as a place where my dreams will become reality, my hopes will become airborne, and my spirit will spread the simple strength of honesty, integrity, and humility.

"I know a few things to be true," Harrison says softly. "Forgiveness, love, and compassion should be given unconditionally. It took me a long time to forgive and love myself, but I'm there now and I'm never going to leave."

As he finishes talking, Harrison smiles and looks around the room. He knows what we all know; this is a safe haven, a place to share the pain of the past, discuss the problems of the present, and reveal our dreams for the future.

Our group is nontraditional. We meet on a random schedule for informal conversation without a 12-step structure or the auspices of a collective organization. Some men find comfort in the plans and patterns of a more traditional program, organization, or institution. It depends on each individual's experience. In the year before I finally quit drinking, I attended AA and NA meetings. I listened to men and women discuss their experiences. Some sobbed and confessed to drinking again. Others sat silently, their arms folded across their chests like angry statues. Many talked about their gratitude for being in a group that gave them support and stability.

In the end, I chose not to continue attending AA meetings.

I've never been very good at joining groups. A few months after I quit drinking, I was lucky enough to learn about the informal meetings I now attend on an occasional basis. I know some recovery authorities frown on this approach, but I believe each individual should find a program or plan that lends him or her support, comfort, and faith.

Like my friend Harrison and the others in my small band of survivors, sharing our stories and our strength is the key to embracing sobriety. I'm blessed to have them in my corner, and I'm proud to be on their side. The mutual love, forgiveness, faith, and compassion that link our hearts are also our bridge to a bright future. We know it's our responsibility to help other men and women find their way out of the darkness when they're ready to make the journey.

I leave the meeting feeling confident and warm, buoyed by the companionship of my small group of survivors and the promise of another day spent living a clean, sober life.

"Good night, John." It's Harrison calling from across the street. "I'll see you soon. Thanks for everything."

I wave and smile. "You're welcome. It's my pleasure."

And for the first time in many years, I realize that I'm saying the common phrase with uncommon conviction. I've made the transition from wounded victim to loving comrade, and I look forward to continuing the traditions of support, admiration, and love with Harrison, the other members of our group, and the strangers I have yet to meet on my new journey.

———

On the way back to my apartment, I stop at Meiner's to buy vegetables, cheese, eggs, milk, the ingredients for a salad. After the meeting, I invited Trevor and his boyfriend to dinner, a light meal of vegetable frittata, fruit juice, salad. It's been months since I cooked anything elaborate, and I want to keep the menu simple so I don't end up with a mess of inedible rubbish on a plate.

Trevor is a new member of my recovery group. He's new in Kansas City, a transplant from Georgia, and we share a lot of common ground: Irish Catholic heritage, a love of Lucinda Williams and Iris DeMent, writing and laughing as much as possible. Trevor's boyfriend, Rudy, is a small man with a huge heart. He stood beside Trevor throughout his battle with the bottle, including three separate monthlong stays at a clinic in Atlanta. When Trevor's sobriety took root, they decided to leave Atlanta and revitalize their life in a new locale. Since Trevor's parents live in a small farming community in central Kansas and Rudy's company offered a lucrative transfer to its regional office in Kansas City, the move was an easy decision.

"Trev and I were talking about you in the car on the way over," Rudy says as they arrive at 8 o'clock. "Curious to know more?"

"Of course," I say, laughing and tweaking Rudy's cheek. "What was it about?"

"It's simple," Rudy says, glancing at Trevor. And then he asks the question that I've been asking myself for the past two years. "Why are you still single?"

———

Dating as a sober man is a challenge. In the past I depended on liquor to fuel my flirtatious side. After a drink or two, I could plunge into a party or walk into a bar and initiate conversations, deliver witty remarks, invite a man to dance, buy someone a drink. It was easy. It was also false. I was operating on anxiety dulled and distilled by Vitamin V. I was miserable, afraid, lonely, and weak. Alcohol made it possible for me to become entangled in situations that were far from healthy and miles from meaningful.

Sobriety has changed everything, especially how I relate in romantic situations. While my exterior then and now may be identical, the interior has been rewired and redirected to produce a man who operates with confidence, courage, vision, security, and a willingness to dive into a journey that will be bountiful, rich, and rewarding.

With each passing month, I imagine I will find a man to love, cherish, respect, and admire. I imagine a man who will be gracious and humble, humorous and strong, romantic and rugged. In my dreams I see myself living and loving in a new way, a healthy way that makes it possible for me to be honest with myself and my mate for the first time in my life.

Despite my dreams, reality is a cruel reminder that dreams demand more than fanciful visions to bear fruit. In the three years since Dylan disappeared, I've met several men who seemed interested in dating and romance. Keith is a banker, Tyler sells Ralph Lauren clothes, Sam cuts hair, Eli works for an international telecommunications company, Warren is a sales rep for an electronics manufacturer, and Dan is a restaurant manager. They are all great guys in some ways, and collectively they personify my ideal mate: funny, successful, intelligent, handsome, sensitive, compassionate, generous, bold, creative, enthusiastic, curious, sensual, kind, and thoughtful.

Until today, it's been a good news, bad news scenario. The good news is that when you combine the qualities and characteristics of the men I've dated in the past three years, you come up with a terrific mate. The bad news is that none of these men possessed all the traits that I seek. And, in fairness, I failed to live up to their expectations as well.

Keith, the banker with the sculptured hair and expensive wardrobe, announced one Saturday as he sat at his kitchen table that I wasn't his soul mate. He wasn't my soul mate either. I moved on. Keith moved on.

I met Tyler through a mutual friend. After a first date

with two chaperons—the mutual friend and her roommate—
we began spending time together. We went to dinner, attended concerts, watched rental videos late at night in his apartment. We talked about our hopes and fears. And we seemed
compatible and content with the promise of our new friendship. Six weeks after we met, I lost my job, depression
replaced my optimistic mood, and Tyler told me he wasn't
emotionally prepared for a relationship.

"I understand," I told him that night in his living room.
"I'll miss you, but I won't forget you."

"Does that mean I'll never see you again?"

"Of course not. I'll be around."

When he called the following Friday night to tell me he
missed me, I told him I missed him too. "But," I said, "that
happens when you stop seeing someone."

I joined Tyler for dinner nine months later, and the
evening was relaxed, friendly, enjoyable. As I watched him
talk, I realized that my sobriety has given me new levels of
maturity, patience, and grace. The frenetic thought patterns
from the drinking days have been replaced with logic and
wisdom. In the past, I would've pined for Tyler for months,
hoping he would return to my life, declare his devotion,
become my partner.

A few months after Tyler's announcement that he wasn't
ready for a relationship, I met Eli. Tall, blond, gregarious,
and adventuresome, Eli is a charmer, a dreamer, a nut. I was
attracted to his spirit, although it was just a few days later
that I realized Eli was far from who I thought he was when
we first met. He delighted in recounting his sexual escapades
to anyone who would listen. While I'm far from inexperi-
enced, I believe in discretion and privacy. When I listened to
Eli recount his conquests as we drove through a small college town near Kansas City, I knew he wasn't the man for
me. And, in turn, I would never be the man for Eli. I moved
on. He moved on. A year later, I learned that Eli had fallen

in love with a lawyer and they were buying a house together in Brookside, an older neighborhood in the middle of Kansas City.

———

Alcohol once made it easy for me to interact with others, yet it retarded my ability to make sound decisions. My romantic history is soaked in alcohol, from the beer I consumed during college to give me the strength I needed to visit my first gay bar, to the Vitamin V that shattered my friendship with Dylan.

I met my first partner in a bar when I was underage and overwhelmed by the possibilities of love and sexuality. I was already drunk when Finn bought me a scotch and water. We talked. We danced. We went home to his apartment and made clumsy attempts at sex on his living room floor. He was attracted to me, and I was desperate for attention and affection.

After that first night in early July, we began an affair that would endure for 15 years, some happy and some not. We lived in two cities, four different residences, two time zones, two area codes. We traveled, we argued, we reconciled. We separated once for a nine-month period when I grew tired of our sexless life and he found it impossible to communicate. We argued, we reconciled, we decided to move from Hoboken, where we'd lived for seven years, back to Kansas City, where we'd met 12 years earlier. We thought the move would help us renew our commitment, rebuild our relationship, regain our footing as a couple.

We were wrong.

Within three years of our return to Kansas City, the distance between us was greater than before. I'd drifted into an affair. Finn lost himself in work and travel, eventually joining a company in Virginia. One late summer afternoon, when

Finn was on the road and my lover had initiated yet another liaison with a married lawyer from the gym, I decided to have a glass of merlot. It seemed inconsequential, a simple decision that would do no harm and would not be repeated. I finished the bottle of wine that afternoon, enjoying the rush of intoxication and the feeling of release that swept through me like a quiet and gentle stream.

The following evening I drank another bottle. I was alone. Finn was still in Virginia. Jordan was either with his boyfriend or the married lawyer. I needed a companion, and alcohol was ready to serve. And enslave. Within weeks I was going to the bars every Friday and Saturday night. I invited Finn to join me, and he would tag along now and then. Some evenings we invited a third man home to our bed, thinking it would add a sexual edge that would reignite the passion we felt so many years before.

The threesomes ignited a slow fire that would eventually end my relationship with Finn and cause a great deal of pain for us both. If I'd been sober at the time, I doubt I'd have suggested we experiment. I doubt I could have convinced Finn to relax his conservative standards. And I don't believe I would have wanted to create scenarios that would lead to a wave of betrayal, anger, and sorrow that would wash Finn from my life and into the arms of another man.

And yet I couldn't stop. I was drinking daily, trying to convince the world that I was happy, content, at peace, while I was actually dying a slow death of depression, loneliness, and rage.

The alcohol river carried me forward that year toward Andrew. With his dark hair, sensual demeanor, and childlike attitude, Andrew was the antithesis of Finn. I was drifting. Andrew was drifting. We collided one night at the Cabaret, introduced by a mutual friend, and began an affair that bled through two years of drunken nights, arguments, hangovers, and reconciliations.

Within a few days after Finn left for Virginia, Andrew was living in my house. Gradually, we became a couple, known for our drunken dancing, our wild arguments, our passionate kisses traded in the dark recesses of the bars that we haunted several nights each week. Six months after we met, Andrew and I attempted to get clean. Although we swore we would remain sober and live a healthy life forever, the good times lasted less than five months. I don't recall the reason, but one day I bought a bottle of wine. I was standing in the kitchen, pouring chardonnay directly from the bottle into my mouth, when Andrew peered through the window and witnessed my duplicity.

He stormed into the house, shouting and gesturing and accusing. I laughed off his excitement and swore it would never happen again. He accepted my apology and we pledged our devotion to a sane and sober life.

We were wrong.

Within weeks we were back on the road to ruin. Drinks at home before going to the bar. Hundreds of dollars invested in our weekly binges. Disastrous arguments and deadly decisions. Emotional scars and physical damage. It was a torturous time, and it ended only when Andrew accepted a new position in Denver. Although I promised to move to Colorado, I never made the journey. I came close once, landing a writing position with a direct-mail firm in Denver, packing my belongings into a U-Haul, driving across Kansas to within 50 miles of the Colorado border.

In the middle of a blizzard, trapped in a small motel with Andrew and my fears, I told him I couldn't do it. I couldn't move to Denver. I didn't want to be with him. It was an ugly day. I was irrational one moment and lucid the next. He was angry, threatening to take my keys and my truck and drive himself to Denver.

In the end, after driving Andrew to Denver, I returned to Kansas City with Finn's assistance. I moved my belongings back into my apartment and began dating a man I'd met the previous summer during the fallout period from one of my drunken arguments with Andrew. The man was Dylan, and we bounced through a roller-coaster romance for nearly a year before my drinking and Dylan's retreat exploded our friendship.

Looking back, I'm thankful that I spent time with Finn, Andrew, and Dylan. I learned lessons during each friendship, and I value the wisdom, romance, and wonderment that I shared with each of them. In the world as I view it today, every life I touch and every life that touches me is an opportunity to learn, to grow, to venture down the road to happiness, contentment, and peace.

———

The word is relatively common, mentioned in prayer and conversation, poems and catalogs, song lyrics and greeting card sentiments. It has seven letters, requires little ink on the printed page, yet holds such vibrancy and resonance for me now that I use it as a mantra. It becomes part of many conversations that begin at one point and lead innocently in a new direction. A remark about the weather results in a long discussion of faith, God, healing. The clerk in a café inquires about a customer's order and finds himself talking about the power of a miracle. A woman seated alone in the reception area of a doctor's office, terrified about the procedure she will face in a few minutes, listens as a stranger's greeting grows to a whispered dialogue about overcoming the unexpected challenges that the universe presents to everyone sooner or later.

When friends tell me about experiences like these, I know that the word is real. I know that it has great power. And I remember the role that it played in my survival, my miracle, my healing.

The word?

Seven letters. A brevity of ink on the page. Volumes of power in its promise.

The word is *believe*.

And I do.

21 / Peace

The fire flickers in the night, sending heat and flame and remnants of fuel into the stars. The ashes weave nonsensical paths up from the pillars of flame into the dark night air. Like snowflakes in reverse, they flutter upward, drunken flecks of powdery residue, the memory of a solid object disappearing into the distance.

I sit on the floor in Mike's living room, watching the fire, waiting for him to finish a telephone call to his parents. I am in love with Mike. He is in love with me. I have never felt this deep bond, not with any romantic connection, family member, friendship. It takes my breath away when I stop and study the spiritual ribbon that binds our hearts in a union of love, respect, admiration, honor, and affection. The union of our hearts is an unexpected gift of my sobriety. Without a clean mind and body, I would be unable to connect on every level as I connect with Mike. Without a clean mind and body, I would be unable to speak honestly, to act responsibly, to embrace the beauty and grace of this new union.

For the first time in years, I am in love.

I am in life.

I am at peace.

And I am renewed in my vigilance to remain on the clean side of the line, to stay sober, to ignore the hushed whispers from my liquid lover as I walk near the liquor department at a store, watch as someone sips a glass of wine in a bar, consider the possibility that my alcoholism was a fluke, that I can drink again, that I'm going to be able to handle it this time.

I am in love.

I am in life.

And I am at peace.

Miracles. Angels. Blessings from the universe. I watch as the ashes of my past regrets, mistakes, indiscretions, and ignorance float and flutter upward, drunken flecks of powdery residue, the record of my drinking daze slipping deeper into the past as I move with steadfast resolve into my future.

I am in love.

I am in life.

I am at peace.

———

"Tell me what it means to be clean." Quinn pauses to light a cigarette. "Why is it so important to you?"

The answer is always on my mind and in my heart. "I love my new life," I tell Quinn. "I love the way it feels when I get out of bed in the morning. I love the fact that I'm in the first truly adult relationship of my life, and that wouldn't have happened without sobriety. I love the way it feels to tell the truth, to honor my commitments, to respect everyone I encounter. It's just amazing."

Quinn smiles and nods. "I keep hearing you use that word," he says. "Amazing."

"It's the only word that fits," I tell him. "My life is amazing. In three years, I've gone from attempting suicide on the loneliest night of my life to embracing the world with open arms. I still make mistakes. I still have emotional roller-coaster rides. And I still fall short of some goals. The difference today is that I know how to respond to the good and the bad in a healthy way."

Quinn draws on his cigarette. "I guess you're right," he says. "That is pretty amazing."

———

Find me. I will wait. Capture my heart. I will capture yours. Take this moment to tell me one secret. Breathe this life into your soul. Angels come when we are ready.

Find me.

———

The sky is gray; the temperature hovers just below freezing. It's a cold Sunday morning in January, and I'm walking to Unity Temple on the Country Club Plaza. In the past five years, I've visited Unity for Sunday services, AA meetings, productions by a friend's puppet troupe, meals in the vegetarian restaurant that occupies part of the building's basement.

I find the services an ideal companion to my personal spiritual quest. Since I quit drinking, I've enjoyed lengthy conversations about spirituality with friends and fellow survivors. I've read books, listened to audiocassettes, rented videos, attended lectures. With each discussion and every new tape, book, or presentation, I've gained greater insight into my spiritual being.

For me, Unity provides a place to replenish my heart,

mind, and spirit. I find great joy in the experience at Unity: the gentle voices joined in song, the thoughts and ideas expressed by a parade of colorful speakers, the community of peace and well-being that surrounds me when I attend Sunday services.

On this particular Sunday in January, I listen as the speaker talks about patience. I know I've developed a keen power for practicing patience in the past three years. I have learned to be patient with myself and with others. I've learned to recognize impatience and haste as triggers from my drinking daze. I've also learned to wait while the frantic pace of the world quiets into a steady rhythm that allows me to make sane and rational decisions. In the drinking daze, I flew into a rage or made irrational decisions every day. Now that my spirit is at peace, I am no longer controlled by impatience and haste.

"Life is a teacher," the speaker says. "And we are its students. The journey of life is easier if it's traveled hand in hand."

I listen to the man's words, recognizing the thoughts and passions in my journey during the past three years. I have learned a great deal, and I have come to appreciate the hands extended to me by a growing band of special souls, angels, and fellow survivors.

"Let us leave here today," the speaker says in conclusion, "with peaceful hearts, peaceful minds, and peaceful spirits."

I walk outside, into the snowflakes that have begun falling during the service. I raise my eyes, feel the soft wet kisses from above, and smile. At last, after so many long years of searching, I have a peaceful heart. After so many mistakes and regrets, I have a peaceful mind. And after so many dark days and nights, I have a peaceful spirit.

―――――

There's a voice on the phone, a call from San Diego. It's Riley, calling to learn more about my new love.

"Why is this new guy so special?" Riley asks. "You've been in love before."

"Not like this."

"So what's the difference?"

I tell Riley that the difference is clarity, connection, peace, respect, admiration, joy. I tell him that I'm experiencing the depth and integrity of unconditional love for the first time as a sober man. I tell him that I may have been involved with other men, but never before have I felt a deep and binding love on every level.

"That's wonderful," Riley says. "You deserve this after all your hard work."

I listen to Riley's compliments and praise. I listen to the voice on the phone, the call from the coast. I listen to the kindness and gentle faith that fills the space between my apartment in Kansas City and Riley's hotel room in California.

I listen. And for the first time in years, I believe. The concept of deserving happiness, peace, and love has been foreign territory for me. The years of self-abuse, doubt, denial, and fear built a hard wall around my heart. Through all the years with Finn and Andrew, through the many months of Dylan's halfhearted affection, I came to consider myself unworthy of another chance at a relationship. I imagined that I'd committed one too many grievous acts in the arena of love and romance. I imagined that my penalty would be a life without a mate.

And now, in the brevity of one telephone call from a dear friend, I find myself acknowledging a new truth: I do deserve happiness.

———

A journey can change direction in one instant. With the decision to turn left or right, proceed north or south, a journey can lead the traveler in a profoundly different direction from that devised at the moment he takes his first step.

I experience the difference on a Wednesday night in early December. I experience the difference the minute I open my apartment door and see Mike's face. I experience the difference when Mike fills my heart with his gorgeous smile.

"Hi, John," he says softly. "I'm Mike."

Indeed, I experience the difference every time I see his face, hear his voice, remember his tenderness, warmth, and humility. As a sober man, I'm able to appreciate the solidity of a balanced relationship for the first time in my life. There are no secret codes, foreign terms needing translation, no mystery or magic. There is only the gentle sound of two hearts beating in unison, two minds sharing common ground, two spirits finding uncommon grace and beauty.

"Hi," I say when I experience the difference on a Wednesday in early December. "It's a pleasure to meet you."

———

As we embrace our new love and begin building a life together, Mike and I spend hours talking. We talk about hope, dreams, ambition, and the future. We talk about failure, fear, anxiety, loneliness, and the past. We talk. We laugh. We learn.

"I'm afraid of being hurt," Mike says. "And I'm afraid of hurting someone else."

My response echoes Mike's message. We are honest in our fear, knowing that confronting it directly is the only way to extinguish its power. For me, the simple act of stating a fear is a new experience. In the drinking years, when I met a new man and attempted to talk about relationships and romance, I was afraid to admit I was afraid. I feared my admission would betray the exterior confidence I projected like a lighthouse on a fog-shrouded shore. It was, of course, artificial bravado. I was a fractured man, and my shattered spirit was reaching desperately for any sign of acceptance. If someone agreed to a first date, it meant I was OK. If he called for a second meeting, it suggested I was winning the game of deception and betrayal. If we began seeing each other on a regular basis, it created the illusion that I could love and be loved like my friends who were enjoying healthy, balanced, loving relationships.

Today, with my new mate by my side, Technicolor pictures replace the monochromatic images from the past. My grim view of tomorrow has been supplanted by the sound of laughter. And my heart balloons with passion, promise, and joy.

In the first few months after I quit drinking, I often lay in the dark and quiet night dreaming of this new life. I would dream of serenity. I would dream of peace. And I would dream of love.

"Find me," I would whisper. "I will wait."

And now, with my new mate by my side, I know that angels come when we are ready, when we've done the difficult work, when we've learned the simplest lessons, when we believe.

———

Starting over is easy. There have been times in the first three years of my new life that I worried I would never reach this new plateau. I worried I would fall short of my goals. I worried I would forever scramble to keep myself from falling back into the darkness of my liquid lover's embrace.

The moment I hear Riley's voice, I realize I am already on the new plateau. I realize I've achieved my goals. At the moment I listen to Riley's praise and congratulations, I realize that the fear and worry I've felt are overwhelmed by the joy and happiness I find in each new sober day. There will always be the temptation to return to the past. But I know

now that I deserve peace, love, happiness, and in making that admission to myself, I also give myself permission to embrace this new life.

———

"You can call me back later if you'd like," Riley says at the end of his call. "I'll be awake for another hour or so."

I tell him I'll wait until he's back home in New York. I tell him I hope he has a successful meeting the next morning. And then I tell him the most important thing I've mentioned during our conversation.

"Thank you for your love and support," I say. "It's the greatest favor anyone can ever receive."

As usual, Riley deflects the kind words. He makes a joke, mutters something under his breath, barks a laugh into the phone.

"I know you don't like to hear it," I say when he finishes. "But I couldn't have made this happen without the foundation you've given me."

There's a pause, a quiet blip. Then Riley says, "You're welcome, friend. If we don't reach out to the people we love, there's no reason to reach at all."

22 / Surrender

"Do you mind if I drink?" Ken asks. "I need a martini."

We're sitting in La Bodega, a Sunday evening in September, and Ken asks the question I've heard repeatedly since I quit drinking. People feel they need my permission or approval before drinking alcohol in my presence. I know they're being polite and considerate, but the inquiry sounds more unnatural than thoughtful.

"Have a martini," I tell Ken. "I'll have my usual."

He orders vodka and vermouth. I ask for coffee. We start talking about movies, a new production at the Unicorn Theater, an author's appearance that I attended last week at Unity Temple. The waiter returns with our drinks. I find myself staring at Ken's martini, imagining the taste and feel of the liquor as it flows down my throat.

The last martini I remember drinking was with Bill a

month before he introduced me to Dylan. We were at the American Restaurant, an elegant eatery overlooking the shops, office buildings, and pedestrian parks in the Crown Center complex. The trees below were bright with white lights as Bill and I sat at the bar, waiting for our table as we sipped a pair of muscular martinis. We got wrecked that night. Martinis led to wine with dinner and more cocktails at Bill's house afterward. The cocktails led to a drunken game of Scrabble. The drunken game of Scrabble led to inarticulate sex in the cold darkness of the bedroom. No bonus points. No triple letter scores. Just Bill asking me to straddle him backwards so he could look at my ass through my white BVDs.

"So it doesn't bother you if people drink in front of you?"

Ken holds his glass between the thumb and index finger of his right hand. He looks like a hybrid of Noël Coward and Shelley Winters, a cherubic curmudgeon with a rapier wit and voluminous laughter. His cheeks jiggle when he smiles and says, "I just don't want to offend you. I mean, now that you're so sparkly clean."

"Now that offends me," I tell him. "If I choose not to drink, it doesn't mean you can't."

Ken sips his martini. "Say you were addicted to sugar or baked goods. Wouldn't it be rude if I ordered dessert?"

"I get your point. I suppose it would depend on each situation. Some people might get uncomfortable if they quit drinking and then spent time around people who were drinking."

"Does it ever bother you?"

"Not really," I say. "If I go out to a club or party, I usually know when it's time to leave."

"And that would be?"

I smile at Ken. "That would be when people start to get loaded. When they cross the invisible line between the real world and insanity."

I remember the invisible line. At least, I remember thinking about it the morning after, when I'd wake with a dull throb behind my eyes and a stale, dry taste in my mouth. I'd wait until the room stopped quivering, and then I'd try to reconstruct the previous evening's events. If only I'd been more aware of the invisible line when I was drinking, perhaps then I could've salvaged some of those nights instead of struggling to piece together a handful of soggy images into a complete picture.

"So you're, like, an expert on knowing when people are loaded?" Ken's voice is sarcastic. I'm surprised by the tone until he grins, and I realize he's joking. "I'm sorry," he says. "I just think it's wonderful that you're OK now. From here on out, it'll be nothing but blue skies, right?"

I wish. Blue skies and big smiles and all the ugly memories swept from my mind and discarded on the far side of the invisible line. If only recovery were like a light switch, a quick flip, and the mind, heart, and spirit are replenished. *Click*. All better now. *Click*. The bad times and broken hearts and bitter tears gone forever. *Click*. Order restored.

I wish. Instead, recovery is a daily process. It's finding the momentum that works. Just as every alcoholic has a favorite beverage, every sober man must find the combination of therapy, spirituality, nutrition, and care that works for his mind, body, and spirit. In the early days of my sobriety, I discover four simple truths about recovery:

Recovery is work. It's remembering the past without poisoning the future. I spend part of every day thinking about the drinking daze. The recollections can be triggered by a movie title, a song lyric, or a snippet of overheard conversation. Many of the memories are ugly and painful, some are amusing, others are tragic. Whenever they appear, I am no longer ashamed or saddened. Instead, I acknowledge their presence and renew my pledge to keep living a life that is defined by grace and humor, goodness and light.

The work of recovery can include private or group therapy sessions, AA meetings, spiritual avenues of inquiry and growth. In my first three years of clean and sober, I've explored a range of options: weekly one-hour conversations with a therapist; occasional sessions with my informal, non-traditional group; books written by psychologists, medical professionals, pop singers, nutritionists, poets, novelists, sociologists; meditation and herbal baths and massage. It doesn't matter what paths I pursue as long as the movement is forward and the mind is free to explore.

Recovery is a challenge. During the first few months of my new life, I was often tempted to go out and buy a bottle of Vitamin V. Why not? Who would know? I could slip away for an evening and return to my liquid lover's arms without detection. Somewhere in the moment of temptation, I found strength. For the first time in my life, I discovered a new strength that came from self-love and self-respect.

When I speak of my recovery, many men tell me they're amazed at my strength and resilience. I respond by telling them that I'm blessed to have a second chance at a sober life. The amazing thing is having the clarity of heart, mind, and spirit to face the challenges of my new world without resorting to the poisonous passion I once shared with liquor. Challenges can be resolved without alcohol, irresponsible behavior, self-destructive choices. They can be tackled with wisdom, compassion, and the clear vision to see that, despite the momentary obstacles or unexpected hurdles, the chosen destination is attainable.

Recovery is constant. For the rest of my life, I will strive for clarity and peace. I will maintain an ongoing vigil to ensure that I stay focused on my new path. Although I learned from my nine-year honeymood that I could live without alcohol, I also know that pride and self-esteem are far greater friends on the journey to a sane, sober life.

Recovery is love. It's sweet and simple; by pursuing a new life, I've discovered the ability to love myself as I am—flawed and tarnished and imperfect. But the love I've found in this new life is far more powerful than any affection I've ever experienced. It is pure. It is bright. It is fierce. It is also forever.

———

On a Friday night in June, I decide to go to the Dixie Belle and the Cabaret, a weekend excursion to my old torture chambers. The rooms seem shabbier, the people more desperate, the atmosphere clouded with lifeless whispers and dull communication. Men reach for youth, adoration, love, attention, affection, energy, death. Men suck poison into their mouths, trying to extinguish the lonely light flickering in their eyes, seeking flesh for fantasy and the promise of going home for the night with someone who is better-looking, better-known, better-hung.

I look around the rooms, the dance floors, the sidewalk sale at the end of the night and I realize I will never forget this world. It will always be a part of my story, a slice of my personal hell. It will always be a part of the past.

———

A few days later, I'm driving west on Shawnee Mission Parkway with Riley. He's in Kansas City for a visit, accompanied by his Nokia, a sheaf of legal documents, and the unmistakable urge to hide from the world and share room-service meals, TV movies, and news updates about mutual friends.

"Let's skip the workout and go back to the hotel," he says.

I give him a frown. "We're going to lift," I tell him. "Then we can go back to the hotel."

"You're so focused now," Riley says with a laugh. "Sometimes I wish you were still drinking. Then I could get you to do almost anything."

I ignore Riley's remark. He stares out the window at the

passing landscape. Then he says, "There are two things we can do when we think we're going to drink again. We can drink. Or we can surrender and learn to love ourselves."

On a bumper sticker, this sentiment would seem insincere. Coming out of my friend's mouth, it sounds reasonable. After nearly three years of clean and sober, I know he's right. In the drinking days, I lost my way in a blaze of alcohol and addiction. Along the way, I met amazing men, shared incredible experiences, broke some hearts, had my heart broken, learned a few lessons, passed along wisdom and advice and encouragement. In the end, I forgot the most important part of living a healthy life: I forgot to love myself.

———

I call Jake on a damp and dreary Sunday afternoon in early October to see if he wants to meet for coffee. I'm standing in the kitchen when the doorbell rings. I open the front door of the apartment, peer around the corner to see who's ringing the bell. It's Dylan, dressed in khakis, a plaid shirt, a timid smile.

"I have a visitor," I tell Jake. "Can I call you back?"

When I open the front door to the building, the wet chill sweeps in and around me. I smile at Dylan and invite him inside. I notice an envelope in his hand. My birthday is tomorrow, and I realize instantly that Dylan decided to hand-deliver the greeting rather than send it through the mail.

"How are you?"

He tells me that he's fine, that his cousin is getting married and he had to shop at Pottery Barn and thought he would just drop by with the birthday card. It's good to see him, but the unexpected visit makes me nervous. I fumble for a brief moment and then begin to ramble: talk of new books, a play that Dylan saw recently at a local theater, the weather, a friend's move to Florida.

This conversation is like so many others we've had in the past three years. We talk in polite sentences about other people, intangible subjects, movies and books and music and plays. During the brief time that Dylan is in my apartment, I can barely look at him without wanting to touch his hand, kiss his lips, hold his heart in my embrace and tell him that I'm sorry.

I'm sorry.

I'm so, so sorry.

But I've already said those words. He knows I'm sorry. And we both know that the brief moment in time when our hearts were united is long ago and never to be again. Despite the proof of life in my eyes and voice, I don't know if Dylan will ever believe that I'm a changed man, that alcohol is no longer a threat to my life, that I healed the holes in my heart.

The minute I saw him standing outside in the cool mist, my heart exploded. It happens whenever I see him or when I talk with him. I have come to accept that there's a chance that a small part of my heart will always be in love with Dylan, and I wonder about the twisted emotion of this experience. After nearly three years of forced friendship and polite dinner conversations, how can I still love the one man who walked away from me?

I like to think that if I had known Dylan would walk out of my life that Sunday, I would never have tumbled into an afternoon of Vitamin V and smoking and laziness. But it's impossible to know. At that moment on a sunny Sunday afternoon in April, I was the first to walk away from the relationship. I had walked away many times before that day. I was juggling two lives and two lovers, and I thought I could maintain the charade without detection or consequences.

I could not have been more incorrect.

No one can successfully maintain a dual life of sobriety and active drinking. I'm sure some men claim to succeed with duplicitous existences, but I question their assertions. At some point, on some sunny Sunday morning, the cards will tumble, the cracks will widen, and their universe will be altered forever.

It sounds dramatic, a storyline from a movie about addiction, the propaganda of someone who no longer spends time with the two lovers who once meant so much to him. But I say these things because I have paid the price and endured the journey and now choose to do whatever I can to help other men with their struggle.

Looking back at my life, I know which choices were made from a place of clarity and conscience and which choices were determined by addiction and hedonism. I can't erase the past. I can only accept it. And in accepting the years that have passed and the actions that have transpired, I know I have a clearer vision of who I will be during the second half of my life.

I will be a man with a clear mind and a cloudless heart. I will make mistakes. I will experience lust and laughter, jealousy, rage, anger, sorrow. I will be a friend, a teacher, a traveler. Alone and with loved ones, I will ride destiny's waves and cherish each new day.

———

A few minutes after Dylan leaves, I open the birthday card he brought to my door. The cover is a photograph of a mist-shrouded lake at dawn. The image reminds me of new beginnings, and the sentiment inside echoes the thought. It is a quote by John Muir: "One can make a day of any size and regulate the rising and setting of his own sun and the brightness of its shining."

Beneath the quotation, in Dylan's strong and sturdy script, is another message: "You've made this true for you. I'm still working on it for myself."

At that moment, as I reread the card, I want to take

Dylan in my arms and pepper his cheeks with soft petal kisses. I want to tell him I love him still, as a friend now instead of as a lover. I want to thank him for the role he played in my sobriety. And I want to tell him that everything in his life will be OK, that he will find true love, that he will discover happiness around a corner on the road ahead.

I climb into bed and turn off the lights. I close my eyes, conjure his face in the darkness. I know I can't hold him, can't kiss him, can't share my friendship and affection. Instead, in the silence and shadows of this overcast afternoon, I can do nothing more than send thoughts of love and peace in his direction. We were once bound by an imperfect love. Now we are linked by fading memories of a failed and fragile romance.

In the silence and shadows, I pray for Dylan and close another chapter from the drinking days.

Adieu, gentle man.

Farewell, beloved.

Good-bye, dear heart.

23 / THE WARNING SIGNS OF HAPPINESS

I'm sitting in Quinn's kitchen, watching him boil water for tea, listening to him chirp and chatter about his new outlook on life.

"You'll start to feel comfortable with everything at some point," Quinn says. "Just when that happens is anyone's guess. I think some people plug in immediately. It took me a year to believe I'd made it across the line into the safe zone."

He turns to look at me, a radiant smile on his tanned face, a glow of contentment in his eyes. I'm beginning to recognize the warning signs of happiness, and the growing awareness is creating an entirely new form of anxiety. I came to Quinn's to hear his advice on recovery and sobriety. With many years of clean living, I hope he will reveal some mystical secret, a magical code that will make it possible to fully engage myself in the pleasure I'm discovering in my new world.

"What are you thinking?"

I know he's looking for a clue, some sense of the mad swirl in my mind. My face always betrays my interior, projecting appearances and personas that frequently have no connection with my thoughts or intentions.

"I'm thinking that I have to learn to give myself permission to be OK with all of this," I say, sputtering the sentence like a spray nozzle on a garden hose. "I'm not used to feeling good. I'm not used to being confident. It's all so strange."

Quinn moves the teakettle from the burner. With methodical movements, he unwraps two tea bags, arranges them in a pair of cinnamon-colored cups, floods the empty vessels with a rush of boiling water. Then he swivels around and wags one finger in the air.

"Well, you know, you have a lot to learn about being sober. Starting with the fact that it's OK to be happy."

———

When you spend a lifetime perfecting the art of sorrow and sadness, happiness is a foreign concept. It is something that blooms in other hearts, certainly not in a soiled life laced with deception, anger, loneliness, and fear. During the drinking days, I spent half the time wanting to be *somewhere* else and the other half of the time wanting to be *someone* else. My life was a blaze of forsaken identity and misfortune: wrong time, wrong place, no turning back, slippery when wet, danger, proceed with caution.

I ignored the signs. I gunned the engine, lit the fuse, jettisoned the lifeboats and oxygen masks and any other instruments of logic and practicality. I turned my back on civility. I raced into the wind, walked on the edge of nothingness, hovered above a dark and murky future, tempting fate and teasing the fortunes. I ignored every signal my intellect broadcast to my heart and soul. I slammed the gas pedal, increased the speed, closed my eyes to the light and crossed without looking in either direction. I laughed when others cried, and cried when there was no possibility that a witness might see my tears, hear my heart breaking, offer succor and sanctity for my lifeless spirit.

When you spend a lifetime dreaming only nightmares and breathing only fire, fury, and rage, the concept of happiness is alien. A thick curtain hangs between reality and the private hell that encases the senses. Logic cannot take root. Honor can find no firm ground on which to grow. There is only the dark night, the hungry shadow, the fear and loneliness and isolation that breed an endless army of negative thoughts, irrational actions, illogical conclusions.

For nearly 40 years I was a prisoner in my own penitentiary of poison and dread. I was a captive, a sacrifice, a ghost. I was identical to the hundreds of thousands of men who came before me and those who are currently drowning in the ocean of alcohol that seduces each thirsty spirit into a deadly dance of denial and fear and rage.

When you spend a lifetime swimming in an empty ocean, you lose hope, compassion, optimism, and pleasure. You lose sight of tomorrow. You drift and waver and float somewhere between the past and the future, a ravaged traveler lost on the dark and murky current.

For nearly 40 years I rode the waves of lies and deception that liquor helped me create. I sailed the sour seas, lost and lonely and searching for a safe harbor, a haven, a home.

I am one of the lucky survivors. I look ahead now to a life of clean and sober, a life of love, passion, trust, faith, and honesty. I look ahead. I do not look back. I know what is behind me, and I know what I will do with today. The future is uncharted territory, and I anticipate the possibilities and relish the mystery with a keen sense of thankfulness. I survived what consumes others. I survived what chokes life from the hearts and spirits of many men during the moments it takes for me to write this sentence. I survived so that I can hold out a steady hand to another and say the words that Quinn spoke to me so many months ago.

"It's OK to be happy."

———

Alone in the morning, the white light of day draining through the curtains and flooding my room, I see the past clearly. It is over. It is done. I survived, carrying scars and regrets and half-remembered scenes of disgrace and disillusionment. I see the connection that runs between surrendering to temptation as a child and swallowing the lies as an adult. I view the events and individuals without a filter. They stand in stark contrast to the present day and future promises, grim sentinels guarding a vault of desire and damnation.

I have paid my debts. I have apologized. I have searched for forgiveness and redemption. Whatever my critics may say about my past indiscretions, I can only say that I survived addiction, not to shy away from responsibility but to acknowledge the roles played by both myself and my liquid lover.

It was a conspiracy of fear, a landslide of weakness, a wave of learned behavior that swept my spirit far from shore and submerged my heart in a wasteland of arrogant and selfish pursuits. I am human. I failed once. I will fail once more. But I pledge that I will never again dance with the same demons that caused me to drown in a pool of Vitamin V and nearly end my life on that night in early April so many years ago.

My debts are paid. My apologies are delivered. My heart is light and alive. I am free to go.

———

An E-mail from Riley: "We may win this war. We may lose. The honor is not in how well we fight or the power of our weapons. The honor is how high we hold our heads during battle."

I write my response late on a moonlit night: "Are you OK? I'm concerned about the military images and talk of weapons. What's up? I'm feeling so free these days. I went to the theater with friends last night to see a play about fairies and dreams and wishes that come true. It made me think about you. So funny that you wrote today. How's work? How's play? I miss you."

Thirty minutes after I send the note, Riley replies: "No worries, mate. All will be forgiven. All will be explained. Time is short. Memories are long. Would you like a twist or an olive in your martini?"

Not funny. He's making no sense. I reach for the telephone, dial his number, listen to the recorded greeting. His voice is flat, airless. The words are dry, stitched together with little gasps, the intake of breath. He says, "I'm not here right now. Actually, I'm not anywhere right now. Please leave a message if you care to, though I'm not certain anyone will return it. We're far too busy being far too busy to do much more than stay far too busy."

The message is obtuse and infuriating. I call Riley's sister. She tells me it's been months since they talked. She tells me he hasn't returned her calls or responded to her notes. She tells me she's worried.

When I ask why she hasn't taken a cab across town to find out if he's OK, she says, "Well, you don't know anything about my life, now do you?"

———

Everyone has an opinion about the definition of happiness. There are academic points of view, scholarly treatises and studies and documents sewn together with crisp language and charts and graphs. There are theories developed by psychologists, threads of wisdom woven into concrete statements of fact.

And there are uncommon stories of clarity, the words and sentiments and scenarios expressed by survivors to tell their truth. Happiness is laughter and a pure white blanket of fresh snow and a dog's sloppy wet kisses.

Happiness is a moment in time, a recollection from the past, the promise of a future event unfolding as planned. Happiness is sunshine, glorious music, the sound of a clear stream coursing through a mountain meadow. Happiness is accessible. It is also hidden. Happiness is a heart beating with strength and joy. Happiness is healing a wound, mending a broken relationship, holding a hand toward a friend in need or a stranger in distress. Happiness is holding Mike in my arms, sharing our hopes and dreams, exploring the mystery that is love. Happiness is dinner with friends, an evening filled with conversation and laughter and the language of trust and faith.

Happiness is finding peace in my progress as a recovering alcoholic. Happiness is admitting my fears. Happiness is knowing I can walk through them without losing sight of my destination. Happiness is knowing that Mike and I have endured many empty, lonely nights to embrace the precious moment of today and anticipate the unspoken pledge that our love, trust, and faith will continue to unfold with each passing day. Happiness is calling my friends to tell them I care. Happiness is indulging my childlike spirit when it needs to play, accepting the responsibilities of adulthood, finding time and space to pray for those who are without shelter, food, funds, hope.

Happiness is living in peace without fear, releasing fear without anger, relinquishing anger without injustice, and accepting the injustices of the world with peace. With a joyful heart and a reawakened spirit, it becomes possible to accept happiness as the result of my new clean and sober life.

———

It is midnight, a Friday night in February. In the night sky above, in the dark curved bowl that captures the promise of an evening to dream and rest, the moon glows like a lantern, like a balloon burning from within to illuminate the traveler's imminent steps.

I look at the clock again. It's been a long day and I am exhausted, but I'm also somehow unable to sleep. Mike is in Detroit, a business trip, a five-day delay between our skin touching as we sleep, between the taste of his kiss, between the hushed and radiant murmur of our voices in the still morning air.

"Good night, sweetie," he said earlier, during our second telephone call of the evening. "Get some sleep."

I know I will sleep, but it will have to wait until later, at some point between now and the rising of the sun on Saturday morning. I will sleep, but first I want to wrap my arms around the happiness that this new love has brought to my life.

"It's amazing," I say to friends when describing my new-found freedom to embrace a new relationship. "I can't believe how it feels. I've never been so happy in my life."

As the words leave my lips, I'm struck by the cliché, the trite sound of the phrase, the pedestrian rhythm of the language. And yet, in the instant I analyze the sound of my sentence, I also know I am absolutely correct.

"I've never been so happy in my life," I say again. "For the first time, I'm fully engaged. I've connected on every level because every level is functioning. I'm blessed and grateful. It's just amazing."

———

Find me. I will wait. Capture my heart. I will capture yours. Take this moment to tell me one secret. Breathe this life into your soul. Angels come when we are ready.

Find me.

———

A long time ago, shortly after I survived the suicide attempt and the insanity of my drinking ceased, I remember thinking that love would be forever elusive. I remember thinking that I would live a single life, that I would be the eternal first-date candidate who never received a second invitation. I resigned myself to the fact that happiness and love would exist on opposite sides of an invisible wall, never joining forces, never combining energies, never allowing a glimpse of the treasures that await a healthy heart, mind, and spirit.

———

"Here's the reason I called," Quinn says. "I wanted to say that I found the book I was talking about earlier, but it was the wrong book. It didn't have the quote about perceived happiness being the something-something of eternal love. I must've made that up somewhere along the line. Anyway, just remember that you deserve all the good things that are happening. It's your time."

I listen to Quinn and I think: *If it's my time, it's taken long enough to arrive.* He continues describing a book he read on a flight a few months earlier, a self-help guide written by a surgeon from San Francisco. It was a terrific inspiration, a big help, a revelation. And then I think: *If it was so helpful, why can't he remember the name of the book or the exact quote?*

"Thanks for calling," I say when Quinn runs out of steam. "I'll try to track it down at the library or online."

"I'm serious about what I said."

"So am I. I'll look for the book and tell you what I think after I've read it."

"No." There's a granite edge to his voice. "I mean, I'm serious about it being your time. When we get clean, we can continue to carry this sack of shit that makes us believe we're unworthy of good things. I wanted to remind you that you deserve happiness."

And now I'm thinking: *OK, I understand now. Quinn called again to talk about happiness because I need a reminder that it is OK to experience happiness, bliss, unconditional love.*

I thank Quinn for his call and smile when he says, "Thank yourself, buddy. You're making it come true every day that you stay sober."

———

In the early days of my sobriety, I consciously considered the number of hours, days, weeks, and months that had elapsed since the last dance with Vitamin V. I would count the time, smile with pride, wonder with fear if I could add another clean day to the total.

Today, I no longer count the hours, days, or weeks. I occasionally stop and calculate the number of years and months. The difference is that today, I only smile with pride, knowing I'm secure in my sober life and set on maintaining the sanity for the rest of the days that I draw breath.

It's taken nearly three years, but I can now say that I agree with Quinn. I've faced fears that once caused me to escape into a haze of alcohol and mindless sex. I've handled anxiety that once forced me to hide from the world. And I've resisted the temptation to drink again during days that were filled with stress when I lost my job, worried about money, experienced rejection by a potential romance, disappointed myself by failing to meet goals and expectations.

In all the dry days, I've learned one lesson that surpasses all others in this new life. I've learned that I deserve happiness. I deserve love. I deserve peace. And I know that I am making it come true with each new sober day.

Angels come when we are ready. Then again, they may be right here with us all the time, waiting for an opportunity to rescue our hearts, to salvage our spirit, and to show us we are worthy of love and tenderness, trust and faith, joy and happiness.

———

Another late night in February, another glowing moon. I'm reading a magazine, waiting for sleep to arrive, thinking about my love and his smiling face. The phone rings. Quinn again, my guardian angel of timely reminders, calling to offer one last morsel of advice.

"The minute you stop drinking is the minute your hard work begins," Quinn says. When I remain quiet, he continues. "It's easy to say no to a cocktail," he says, "but it's hard to say yes to a new life."

"Is that a Hallmark card for recovering addicts?"

The silence tells me that Quinn is not amused.

"It sounds like a greeting card," he says finally. "But it's something I wrote in my journal one time. I'd been through some argument with somebody about the really hard part of getting clean. They thought it was quitting booze. I think it's starting to live life without it."

"So how do you make that transition?"

"With care and a plan," Quinn tells me. "That's the beginning of any new life. That's how you reach the place you're dreaming about."

24 / Choices

Clarity can arrive in a well-dressed package. Or it can appear as the shadow of smoke after a fire.

For days after my conversation with Quinn, I carry his comments in my mind, imagining that I will create a detailed plan for my new life that will define my actions, intentions, goals, and aspirations.

There will be a beginning, a middle, an end. Everything will have purpose. Everything will be sculpted from honesty and integrity and devotion to a life of peace and love. I will no longer squander my time and energy on meaningless mayhem. The self-imposed exile of life with alcohol will be replaced by communion with the world. Fear, anxiety, insecurity, sorrow, shame, denial, and all the other negative emotions I've known so well for so long will be banished to far edges of the planet. I will rise above the darkness of my drinking and bathe in the magic of a sober, sane life.

I imagine that my new plan will reveal itself during a dream, a soft moment before dawn, during the tumult of a thunderstorm.

A few days later, I call Quinn to describe my new state of mind. I tell him that I'm working on a plan, that I'm preparing for my brave new world. I describe my intentions and ideas, my expectations and conclusions. I tell him about the clarity that surrounds my heart, mind, and spirit.

"Don't try so hard," Riley says. "Just relax and live your life. Things will fall into place. It just takes time."

I listen to him ramble on about his own experiences. I try to concentrate on what he's saying, but my mind keeps roaming back to one thought: How long? How long will it take before I'm better? Before my mind and heart click into new patterns? Before I feel at home and at peace?

How long?

———

I settle into a new routine. I buy books about healing and recovery, fill my rooms with lively music, learn to spend hours alone. I reconnect with friends, make plans for dinners and the theater and long walks through Loose Park. I sit quietly each evening, reflecting on the day and the choices I've made since morning.

I make lists of tasks and activities designed to create a fresh home environment for my newborn spirit. I paint the walls in my living room, replacing the blank white surfaces with warm ochre planes that embrace and comfort.

Over the course of two or three weeks, I sort through the clothes and books and papers and packages that have overpowered my closets. I drive to the Goodwill store with bags of belongings, items I accumulated during the drinking days in a mad dash to collect more and more because I felt like less and less.

At night, in the stillness of my room, I lie in bed. The past echoes through the shadows as I remember the men who came and went through my life. I can see Andrew's face, the shock and sadness after my fist connects squarely with his jaw. I can feel Finn's patient hand as he steadies me on the day that I choose life and renounce my affair with alcohol. And I can hear Dylan's quiet voice reciting the rosary, as I once asked him to do on a night long ago. "Hail, Mary, full of grace. The Lord is with thee. Blessed art thou among women and blessed is the fruit of thy womb, Jesus. Holy Mary, Mother of God, pray for us sinners now and at the hour of our death. Amen."

As the memory of Dylan's voice fades, I realize that Quinn is on to something powerful. The past is part of the present, a piece of the future, a foundation for all that I do from this moment forward. I must embrace what happened during the drinking daze. I must acknowledge my role and responsibility in the things that were said and done. And, most important, I must forgive myself for my sins.

———

A phone call in the middle of the night: bad news about Harrison. He relapsed, ended up in jail, a third DUI. It started with an argument, a long-distance shouting match with Jason, barking into his cell phone at 2 o'clock in the morning. The argument was about money, the division of a joint bank account, the sharing of the spoils.

"So then he just decided to have a drink," Ian says. "One drink. The next thing you know, he's looking for bail and a lawyer. Not a wise choice."

"Did he try to call anyone?" We all offer support and

friendship at any time, day or night, local, long-distance, collect. "I know he has my number."

Ian sighs. I can hear the weight, the sorrow through the phone. "No," he says. "He just didn't want to be here anymore. He was tired."

––––

If we drink to avoid, to run, to hide, what happens when we quit drinking? I can't sleep after Ian's call. I remember when I felt tired, like I didn't want to be here anymore. It was a Monday night in April, my mother's birthday, the day after Dylan left. I was tired. I was angry. I was alone. And I was drinking.

I roll around in bed, wrestling with the pillows and blankets. At 6 o'clock I make a pot of coffee, watch CNN, wait until 8 o'clock arrives. I dial Harrison's number. He picks up on the second ring.

"Hey, buddy."

He starts to cry. "I'm sorry," he whispers. "I'm so, so sorry."

"What are you doing right now?"

When he tells me he's in the middle of absolutely nothing, I tell him to get dressed. "I'm coming over," I say. "We're going to breakfast."

––––

There is comfort and safety in numbers. As someone who's lived many years as an outsider, I am now a poster boy for the power of friendship, community, and companionship. I know I can pick up the telephone at any point during the day or night and find someone who will listen, someone who cares, someone who will help if I find myself in a dangerous place.

After three years of sobriety, I believe strongly in Quinn's advice: "The minute you stop drinking is the minute your hard work begins. It's easy to say no to a cocktail, but it's hard to say yes to a new life."

In the years since I quit drinking, I've learned to share that wisdom with others. I've learned to provide unconditional love, support, and encouragement. I've learned that the brotherhood of recovery is a powerful tribe. I've also learned that my sobriety grows stronger each time I share my story with someone who struggles with sorrow, trouble, or tragedy.

The brotherhood is not limited to addiction. Some of the men I speak with are burdened by debt, depression, loneliness. When I share my story and offer my love, I'm passing along the support and encouragement that I received from my friends and family during the early days of my recovery. I'm blessed to have had so many angels watching over me: Finn, Andrew, Lana, Anna, members of my family, other men who had survived their addiction and offered unconditional love. Each time I hear someone say they're struggling with addiction, depression, sorrow, or loneliness, I remember my own battle and I'm ready to help in any way I can so they will know they're not alone.

"It takes one to cry," Riley once told me. "But it takes two to begin the healing."

———

Harrison is sitting on the front steps of his house when I arrive. For a handsome man, he looks less than attractive: A Nike cap shields his eyes, his skin looks mottled and dry, brown-and-gray stubble covers his chin.

"Hey," he says when he climbs into my truck. "Thanks for calling. I could use someone to talk to right now."

We drive to First Watch for breakfast. After we order food, coffee, and juice, Harrison stares out the window at the cars coursing along Shawnee Mission Parkway. He's a million miles away, and I watch as the traffic lulls him with its hypnotic flow.

"You want me to start?"

He looks at me and nods.

"What happened?" I pour cream into my coffee and give him a minute to ponder the question. "You'd been sober for what? Six years?"

"Seven." His voice is barely audible. "Seven years last month."

I repeat my question. He stares out the window. We sit in silence until the server delivers Harrison's pile of wheat-germ pancakes and my omelet. I watch as he floods his plate with sticky, sweet syrup. I can smell the maple and butter from my side of the table, and the smile that appears on Harrison's face after his first bite is understandable.

"This was a great idea," he says. "Now I feel like talking."

And he does. He describes the jumble of fear and anxiety that filled his mind after he argued with Jason. "It was a stupid choice," he says. "I'm an idiot for allowing him to make me drink again."

"You are not an idiot," I say, "and you did not allow Jason to make you drink. It was your choice. Stupid or not."

We volley the subject back and forth. I can tell that Harrison feels embarrassed about his relapse. I know the feeling. When I started drinking again after a nine-year dry period, my embarrassment did nothing but add fuel to the fire. I was ashamed I'd allowed liquor to regain its control over my life, yet I was unable to stop. My relapse was sweet, divine agony, and I can see the same look in Harrison's eyes that I once saw in my own. Sobriety demands constant attention and an unwavering desire to remain focused on clarity, health, and sanity. In one moment, with one choice, addiction can sweep back into your life like a conquering army. Harrison is back at the beginning, returned to the initial baby steps of recovery that I know well after my three years of sobriety.

As I listen to him talk about his plans for finding a new therapist, rejoining his AA group, plotting his new life, I remember another important lesson I've learned since I quit drinking: Take nothing for granted. At the beginning of each new day, at the close of each dark night, I remember to thank my angels and honor the love that helped me climb up from the darkness and into the light. Without their love and support, I'm not certain where I would be on my journey. I know my progress is due in part to the power, grace, and wisdom that my friends shared during the early days of my return to civilization.

"So what do you think?" Harrison says. "Feel like taking a walk?"

I smile. "Do you?"

"You bet," he tells me. "I'm ready to try it all over again. Promise to help me if I fall down again?"

The innocent look on his face fills me with emotion and I feel my eyes moisten. "You bet," I say. "I promise to help in any way that I can. Now let's get out of here. This day is too good to spend inside."

———

"I don't know if you remember me," I say when my brother answers the phone on Monday night in January. "I'm your younger brother."

There's a brief pause, a blip of empty air, and he says, "I remember you. What's happening?"

It's been three years since our last conversation. I called him after three years of silence because it's time to extend my hand, to initiate a dialogue, to begin rebuilding the bridge that was swept away during my years of drinking by a consistent pattern of irresponsibility, carelessness, and selfish disregard for my brother's family. Before I slipped off the planet and into darkness, I visited their house frequently for dinner, special events, birthdays, holidays. At some point I began to accept invitations and fail to arrive, sometimes phoning the following day with an empty excuse and a flowery apology. I would regain my footing and attend the gatherings with regularity. Then I went through a period of so-so attendance. I would agree to join them for lunch, dinner, or Sunday brunch, but end up drunk at home, phoning a week or two later without mention of my vanishing act.

After I quit drinking and began to reassemble the pieces of my life, I suspected that my brother and his wife stopped talking to me because my previous behavior had become intolerable. They didn't trust me. Tough life. Tough love. Tough shit.

For a few minutes we trade news: his daughters' progress with college and careers, the plans for one girl's wedding, his wife's professional success with an insurance company. When we've finished the formalities and happy talk, I reroute the conversation to its original purpose.

"I decided to call tonight," I say, "because it's been a long time since we talked. I wanted to talk about what happened."

Another short span of silence. My brother is choosing his words, trying to use the precise logic of a man trained in architecture and engineering. Finally, he says, "I'll just lay it out straight. We got tired of you not showing up or calling at the last minute to say you weren't coming over. I'd finally just had it. I decided that when you were ready to call us, we'd be here."

I feel validated; my theory was correct. In one instant I'm flooded with a warm wave of peace, grateful I had picked up the telephone and called my brother. The feeling isn't new. In the three years since I quit drinking, I've made many of these calls. Reaching out to those I've disappointed, harmed, ignored, or offended is a crucial part of the healing process. This call to my brother is one of the final steps. I'm almost home.

"I don't know how much you know about alcoholism," I say when my brother finishes, "but I was in pretty bad shape then. Drinking has a tendency to make you behave in ways that are less than attractive or desirable."

A third pause. "I know about alcoholism," my brother says firmly. "I grew up with it."

The reference to my father's drinking is unexpected. It was always the silent member of our family, something never discussed, something intangible that sent sharp spasms of pain, anger, and resentment through our household. For years I ignored the fact that I had observed my father use alcohol as his ticket to escape the demons that shadowed his footsteps. Hearing my brother talk about it now feels nearly sacrilegious. Our father has been dead for 16 years. Drawing him into a conversation about something that happened between my brother and me doesn't seem relevant. And then it hits me. Our father's alcoholism is absolutely relevant, the core of what we're discussing. My brother's voice still brims with bitterness and anger 16 years after our father took his last breath on a summer night in upstate New York.

I wait for a moment, gathering my thoughts and sorting through the fragmented images of my father. Then I say, "Well, I don't want to talk about that now. I just wanted to apologize for my behavior and let you know I've been sober for three years. I hope you'll forgive me for acting poorly toward you and your family."

And he does. In an avalanche of short, brusque sentences, my brother says that everything is forgiven. He suggests we meet soon. He says he'd like to do that very much.

"So would I," I tell him. "So would I."

———

On every journey there is a moment when the destination comes into view for the first time. An unexplored shoreline observed from a boat on the sea, the pinpoint of light at the end of a tunnel.

As I continue to heal and learn during these first years of sobriety, one destination is in view. After a lifetime of regret, perceived failure, sorrow, and missed opportunities, I'm living a life on the bountiful shore of a new land.

With forgiveness, honesty, integrity, and self-love, I've discovered how to create a way of living based on balance, health, and spiritual well-being. I've learned to accept certain fragile parts of my personality as proof that I'm human. In the drinking daze, the trigger emotions—hunger, anger, loneliness, and fatigue—ignited an alcoholic blaze that could burn for days. I was afraid to feel anything I didn't understand or couldn't control. I was afraid to admit or embrace anything that suggested my inadequacies, ignorance, or faults, thinking they would confirm that I wasn't good enough, smart enough, attractive enough, whatever enough.

I was afraid.

But I am no longer that man.

I am no longer afraid. When I share my story—talking with men who are in recovery or those who seek a clear and sober life—I'm proud of my strength and ever more certain my choice was correct.

I am no longer afraid. The concept of fearless living is now a reality. I move through each day with care and consideration, reaching for new levels of communication, trying to weave one responsible and rational decision, action, and intention into the next. I look at everything with a vision that helps me define myself and decipher the expectations other people have when I interact with them. The change in perception is essential to success with sobriety. Looking at old patterns of behavior with new understanding comes from hours of analysis, either with a therapist, a group, or the self-help books that address each possible permutation of every possible topic.

I am no longer afraid. I never imagined that finding my place in the world would give me such confidence. I always thought I would be that small boy on the playground, the unwanted visitor, the nuisance, the failure. I always imagined that I would be a weak and fearful observer, watching the world spin, wishing I could consume the same pleasures my friends and family members claimed as their own.

I am no longer afraid. When I speak the words, they are no longer a distant destination. They are my fabric and my foundation, the essence of my new life as a sane, sober man.

I am no longer afraid. When I speak the words, my heart fills with gentle pride and a softly beating contentment.

I am no longer afraid. I'm where I wanted to be all along.

I am no longer afraid to make choices.

And I know the choice I will make, now that I am clean and clear and happy.

I want to go home, to the center of my spirit, where I can create a blend of balance, light, energy, joy and hope. In conversations with friends and other sober men, I hear the yearning for home. There is a collective cry for peace, for a place where the pain of the world is replaced by compassion, acceptance, and unconditional love.

During the drinking years, it was easy to avoid this precious place. I wanted to maintain the chaotic pace of my addiction for one simple reason: It was comfortable, familiar. It was ground zero for my flight from dealing with life on life's terms. If I flooded my body with Vitamin V and surrendered to addiction, I could ignore fear and insecurity. I could turn away from my perceived failings and embrace a deep nightmare of dark clubs and casual sex and instant gratification. If I added the correct combination of liquor and pills to my anxious mind, I could escape into a blissful nothingness where I was safe.

Until the next morning.

Until the high was replaced by lows that dipped into a

shadowy abyss of self-hatred, disgust, and shame.

Until the truth was apparent, the fear was revealed in its full force, and I could no longer escape or run or hide.

Until I fell hard against the unwavering reality that is addiction. It was never pretty and rarely pleasant, but I learned to ride the swelling tide of terror and heartache. I learned to stay flexible and keep moving. Moving to avoid contact or detection. Moving to avoid the truth.

I was addicted. I was making choices that were unhealthy, imbalanced, destined to ignite a firestorm that reduced the jagged edges of my existence into a wasteland of woe and dread.

And yet, with hope, strength, inspiration, and the loving support of my family and friends, I learned to reverse the tide, to turn away from darkness, to embrace a life filled with healthy choices, a positive attitude, and the knowledge that I may stumble and fall along the path, but I will never lose hope or direction.

In one moment on an afternoon in April, I make a choice. I choose life. I choose love. And I choose light. They were around me throughout the drinking days, but I refused to see them. I refused to believe I was worthy of love, peace, and grace. I refused to forgive myself and others, a refusal that allowed the deadly embrace of alcohol to remain tight around my heart and spirit.

In one moment on an afternoon in April, I made a choice: life, love, light. It is a choice that everyone who struggles with addiction can make. The miracle can happen to anyone willing to examine his life and the choices that are available. Hopelessness, doubt, shame, humiliation, anger, fatigue, and the other negative forces that swirl through the world can delay the choice and make it difficult to believe there is a place of peace and love. To believe that mistakes and errors will be forgiven. To believe that we all deserve a life filled with balance, light, energy, joy, and hope.

In one moment on an afternoon in April, I choose life. And by making that choice I also dedicate myself to sharing the message of hope and positivity that allows me to continue walking down the sober road.

In one moment on an afternoon in April, I find the one thing I longed for throughout the drinking days.

I find my way home.

25 / HOME

"Where do you want to go?"

Quinn's eyes are bright; his smile beams across the room. We are sitting in a hotel room near the Kansas City Art Institute, a sun-splashed suite that Quinn rented when he decided to return to the Midwest from a 10-year adventure in Los Angeles. He's been looking for a house to buy, finding everything either too small or too big, nothing quite the correct size.

"Do you want to see a movie? We could walk through the Kemper Museum? Go to Loose Park?" He unrolls a long list of optional destinations, presenting a broad range of possibilities. Then he opens the newspaper and begins to recite from the listing of weekend events. "There's a play at the university, a lecture on China, or there's a hockey game," he says, slowing his speech as he reaches the end of the list.

"Kansas City against Montreal. A gallery opening for a ceramic artist." He stops and closes the paper. "Or we could just sit here and stare at the walls."

I know where I want to go. It's the place I go when I want to share a quiet moment, mend a wound, calm my heart. The place I find shelter, warmth, comfort, and love.

The place I call home.

"Let's go to my apartment," I say. "I'll cook dinner. We can play Scrabble or backgammon. Just hang out."

Quinn's smile tells me that he agrees with the plan. "Good idea," he says. "I'm tired of this hotel room."

He stands, extends his hand, pulls me up from the sofa and outside into the warm summer air. We walk to my truck, and I feel serenity envelop me as I realize that I'm finally reaching the part of my journey where the hard work is showing promise. There are evident results from the time I've spent easing myself out of the chaos and into the light.

"This will be a good weekend," Quinn says. "I'm so glad I came back home."

I start the truck, turn into the street. "Coming home is good for everyone," I say. "I'm glad you made the choice to get back to where you belong."

———

And so I am home. After three decades of wandering, I have found my place in the world. I have also found the man who will resuscitate my heart, breathe new love into my life, fill my day with dreams of his beautiful smile and compassionate heart.

I'm smart enough about love to know there are no guarantees. There are only the pledges of respect, admiration, support, love, trust, and truth. In my three-decade journey, I have met many men for dinner, drinks, a day of bike riding, a night of sex. I have tasted the bitterness of rejection and drowned in the sweetness of infatuation. I have transcribed phone numbers from soiled cocktail napkins into my address book, only to discover the digits a few years later and strain my mind trying to conjure an image of the name associated with the number.

It was a bleak existence for many years, a dim pulse of life's true fervor monitored from time to time to ensure that death did not eclipse the promise of a brave new day. I was a cartoon of a man engaged in the commerce of romance and art and professional pursuits, a caricature created to mask the sad and broken heart of a 10-year-old boy who never learned to live in the real world until 30 years later when he was an unshaven, soiled man crawling from his bed to the bathroom, huddled over the white porcelain toilet, staring at the black and white tiles on the floor, praying for deliverance from the chaos that had become his life.

———

Angels arrive when we need them, when we are ready for miracles, when we are ready for dreams to come true. Some angels are messengers; others are guardians and guides. In the first three years of my new life, I meet many angels. Each is a blessing, an aspect of the miracle, a thread in the rope that connects hope to humanity, truth to integrity, wisdom to the heart.

———

His name is Sam. He tells me he is 39 when we meet. He tells me he is another sober survivor. He lived his early years in South Carolina, traveled throughout Europe as a young man, moved to Kansas City at the age of 36 to be near his elderly father.

After an initial conversation in an online chat room, we

agree to meet at Latte Land, the coffee bar two blocks from my apartment. I arrive early, buy my drink, wander outside to wait for Sam. Even though I have been looking for a true partner, a soul mate, an angel, I have no preconceptions about this meeting; it is another man, another night, another name.

For 15 years, I thought that partner was Finn. In retrospect, we were good together for many reasons but never destined to be lifelong mates. I've recounted the story to so many friends over the years that I grow weary when I think about telling someone new why my old relationships failed. It wasn't purely my addiction. Nor was it simply a matter of incompatible halves trying to create a whole. Each man was a miracle; every event taught me an important lesson about myself.

All so I would be ready when I met a man who was my equal.

A man who shares my common ground and believes in respect, support, love, lust, and adventure.

A man with a gentle heart, a warm smile, a compassionate soul.

I've been looking for that man for nearly three years when Sam walks up on a humid Tuesday evening in late August and says, "John? I'm Sam. It's nice to meet you."

———

I am surrounded by memories, fragments of the past, boxes filled with snapshots, old address books filled with names and numbers of long-forgotten tricks, subway tokens, maps of Flagstaff and Phoenix and Nashville and New York. I have diary entries that detail erotic nights and desperate days.

There is no sorrow here in my rooms. I am never alone. Ghosts walk through my nightmares. Angels fly through my dreams.

Finally, after 30 years of clawing through the crevices of

the night, I have become the man who once existed only in my mind. I am at peace with the past, comfortable with the present, excited about the future.

I am lucky.

I am blessed.

I am home.

———

"You can't write about that stuff," Riley whispers. "It's too personal."

I'm not sure why he's whispering. We're alone on the bridge above Brush Creek, two men talking and walking through a still and dark winter night. When Riley called earlier, I was writing and he'd asked to interrupt because he was lonely and frightened and afraid he would drink. He'd resurfaced a few weeks earlier, calling from New York to explain his recent disappearance as another case of the blues. Now he was in Kansas City for a brief visit.

"I was down," he'd explained earlier on the phone. "So I decided to travel for a few days. I called you once from Tampa. So you wouldn't worry. Your line was busy, and I got involved with something before I could try to call again."

I've heard this story before. I've probably told this story before. It's extracted from the dialogue of drinking, the incomplete sentences and inarticulate sentiments that drinkers erect to shield the truth from the light.

I listen to Riley's travel stories for a few minutes. Then I do what I always do when a brother calls for help. I agree to see him. I suggest we meet outside Williams-Sonoma so that we can walk until his fear subsides and his mind is redirected to a healthy alternative.

"Do you feel like dancing?" I ask, suggesting another option beyond the snow-covered sidewalks around The Country Club Plaza. "We could go to the DB."

"I hate that place," Riley whispers. "I've always hated that place."

"But that's where I met you," I say. "Isn't that one good thing that happened there?"

Riley pulls the collar of his coat toward his face. He burrows beneath the gray flannel, cursing the cold and the depression that is draped across his shoulders. Riley is a dear friend, another gentle heart tormented by feelings of inadequacy and failure. We've talked for years about his addiction, which he frequently transfers from alcohol to sex to cocaine to gambling in an attempt to prove he can keep things under control. I've tried to describe my newfound freedom from the tedious and troubling life of addiction, but he wants me to promise that he has no problem because he stays only briefly in the abyss of one substance or behavior.

"I'm not really an addict," he says softly. His breath plumes in streams from his mouth, freezing his declaration in the night air. "My father drank for years, and he never went for treatment. He's doing fine today."

Riley's father is a rare survivor. He should've died many times in many cars along many dark country roads. The accidents and police reports and insurance settlements are concrete testimony to the fact that Riley's father is a lucky man whose plump bank accounts and respected name rescued him from the legal entanglements that would strangle most people who repeatedly engage in drunken driving and one-car accidents.

I think about Riley's father for a few minutes and then suggest that we go to my apartment. Riley shakes his head and tells me he's feeling better. He promises to call me later, after he's back at the Ritz, tucked safely in bed.

"Thanks for coming to talk," Riley says, knotting a royal blue scarf around his throat. "I feel much better now. Thanks for being my friend."

We've had this conversation a million times. I know that

Riley's path will lead from the wintry landscape along Brush Creek to a bar stool at the Cabaret. In the morning he'll call to complain about his hangover and the mindless sex he shared with a stranger and the mess his life has become in the past few years. He'll tell me that he loves his wife yet lusts for the taste and touch of a man. He'll describe the exquisite torture that twists his heart into a knot, kneads his spirit into a hopeless shadow. Then he'll plead with me to talk again, to discuss a solution, to consider the options that life presents when our addiction pulls us into a small, narrow hole in the dark.

I can't rescue Riley. I can't rescue Tony or Mark or Gwen's husband or the investment banker from Tulsa or the man who left his career in real estate to enroll in computer classes at the university.

I can't rescue anyone, but I can show them an example of salvation. I can listen to their words and suggest options for their future. I can tell them how amazing it feels to be home, to be free, to be clean and sober.

And I hope this might help them as others helped me during my dark hours before I came home.

———

I can no longer turn to the wicked combination of Vitamin V and cranberry juice to quench my thirst for pleasure. I have discovered new elixirs to fill my yearning and satisfy my craving in new and unexpected ways.

There are cups of Twinings Prince of Wales tea, chocolate chip cookies, Joan Didion books, and Joan Armatrading CDs. Freshly laundered cotton sheets, the grandeur and drama of a thunderstorm at night, M&Ms, chilled slivers of mango and papaya, Tom Waits's gravel growl, and Billie Holiday's blues. I can revel in HGTV and the History Channel and video rentals and gospel radio programs and reruns of favorite television programs. There are phone conversations with friends in distant cities or across town, dialogue with Mike about spiritual matters and the serenity of sobriety.

———

After dinner at the Classic Cup in Westport, Sam drops me off in front of my apartment. It is late, nearly midnight, and we are both exhausted. I lean over and brush his lips with a slow-moving kiss. Our eyes linger in a long embrace. There is no sound.

"Are you busy tomorrow night?" Sam whispers.

I have no plans, only the intention of seeing him again to learn more about his heart, spirit, and mind.

"Yes, I'm busy," I say. And then I lean nearer. "What are we doing?"

———

I do not intend to fall in love again. I intend to maintain a rigid and steady momentum that will take me from today to tomorrow, that will take me through a myriad of mannequins dressed to resemble human beings, that will take me from one lonely moment to the next.

I do not intend to fall in love again. I intend to protect my heart. I intend to spend time with friends, to travel west for long weekends with Brian in the desert outside Santa Fe or east for holidays with Talbot and Tru in their penthouse a few blocks below Wall Street. I intend to nourish my spirit with solitude. I intend to fill the solitude with celebrations of my survival. I intend to survive by not falling in love again.

I do not intend to fall in love again.

And then I realize it's too late. It's already happened. I'm in love with the man who will make tomorrow brighter, the man who will remind me when I've stepped off the path of humility and light, the man who will seek forgiveness when he fails, the man I wanted to be during all my years of drinking.

I've found the man. After more than 40 years of searching, I've discovered the man I can love who will make it possible for me to love others. After 40 years of feeling disconnected and alone, I've met the guy who will make it possible for me to have a true loving relationship with a life partner. After 40 years I've found the man, I'm in love, and I am home.

I am that man.

After four decades, I discover that the cliché is true. We can't truly love another person until we love ourselves. Despite the years of insecurity and failed relationships and drinking and dysfunction, I've reached the point on my life's path where I can look in the mirror and love the man who's looking back at me. I know I'm human, I make mistakes, I may fail when I try something new. I know I seek forgiveness when I offend or anger another person. I know I have learned the lessons from the dark days and moved into a bright, new place in the world.

I also know that I will continue to evolve and grow as the years pass, because the decision to quit drinking was the first step in a long journey of self-discovery and healing. In the three years since that day, I've longed for a loving relationship with another man, but it took several failed attempts before I met another man who truly matched my heart's desire. For a brief moment, I thought the man was Sam. I also thought the man was Tyler, Keith, Eli, Warren, and Dan.

In the end, it was none of those men.

My love is a man named Mike, a gentle, sweet, compassionate soul who touched my heart with his humility, passion, fire, and yearning for growth. Mike is from Nebraska, the son of proud parents, a loving brother to three sisters, a compassionate and generous soul. When we meet, I sense immediately that he is a beautiful companion for my heart and spirit. He possesses an ideal blend of childish curiosity and enthusiasm. He also possesses the wisdom that is earned through surviving failed relationships, soiled friendships, and life's challenges.

During the early days of our relationship, I discover that I have learned important and valuable lessons in my first three years of sobriety. I've learned to communicate how I feel in a clear manner. I've learned to ask my partner how he feels in a compassionate way. And I've learned to establish and nurture my personal boundaries while respecting those of another.

After four decades of denial and negative thinking and spiritual stagnation, I'm in love and I'm home. It's good to be here. I know there will be new challenges in the days ahead, but I also know I'm ready to handle them in a healthy, sane manner. I can separate fact from fiction, perception from reality, with greater skill and ease than ever before. Knowing I am now capable of dealing with life on life's terms is a crucial step forward. I may still encounter fear, anger, hostility, and jealousy, but I will be ready to respond in a rational way instead of running into the arms of my liquid lover and burying my head in the sand.

I'm in love.

I'm home.

And for the first time in a long time, I'm ready for tomorrow.

———

"I forgot to tell you something."

It's Riley, a few days after our conversation on the bridge above Brush Creek. It's 3 o'clock in the morning, the middle of the night, and Riley's call slices into my sweet dream about walking on a beach in a gentle mist.

"What?"

He tells me that he forgot to tell me he wishes he could

give me a big kiss and a hug. "But like a brother hugs a broth-er," he adds. "I don't want anyone to get jealous or anything. You know? To think there's something between us."

I remind Riley that there is something between us.

"There is?"

"Yes," I say, cradling the receiver against my shoulder. "Love. I love you like a true friend, and I want you to get well. I want you to feel life the way I do."

Riley is silent. I wait for his reply, but he just sits on the other end of the line, taking slow and deliberate breaths.

"You still there?"

He clears his throat to signal he's still with me. Then he says, "I don't think I'm ready. I don't think I can do it yet."

I tell him it's OK. I tell him he doesn't have to decide today or tomorrow. "But you've got to remember I'm here to help you do it when you're ready to quit," I say. "There were people who helped me. And now it's my responsibility to pass on the love to you when you're ready."

A few more quiet words and Riley is gone. *Click*. I hang up the phone, pull the blankets toward my chin, roll into a warm place somewhere between night and morning.

———

I am afraid. I have survived years of addiction, countless dates from hell, the death of my father, my mother's heart attacks and hip replacement surgery, the dissolution of friendships and relationships. I have lost my way in the night. Dylan abandoned me. I abandoned Finn and Andrew. I aban-doned myself. I moved forward, maintained equilibrium, danced on the fragile edge of the night. And I survived it all.

Yes, I am still afraid. I am afraid that I will succeed. I am afraid that I will find happiness. I am afraid that I will always be afraid.

Until the minute I realize that I am afraid. Sounds crazy.

Sounds insane. But on a cool September evening, walking through the Manor Square parking garage after our daily workout, I turn to Ben and say, "We're afraid."

He smiles and says, "Yep. That's it. We're always afraid. It never goes away."

Ben is my neighbor, a trusted friend, a former cocaine addict. He is funny and smart and handsome. He likes baseball and the Dave Matthews Band and Stephen King novels. The apartment that Ben calls home is decorated in Early Bachelor. There's a mounted piranha from his trip to Brazil, a pair of well-worn easy chairs, a pair of mismatched area rugs in the kitchen.

We have become comrades in our journey toward a new life. We talk often about our romantic lives, the joy of sobriety, the terror of the old tapes. And, on this cloudless Tuesday afternoon, our fear.

"I thought it would all get better if I got clean," I say. "But I'm still afraid. I'm afraid I'll succeed. I'm afraid I'll be happy."

Ben nods. "It never goes away."

As we walk through the parking garage toward our cars, I realize that accepting fear as a regular companion is difficult. The old tapes tell us we are doomed to disaster, programmed to perish. Our hearts are comfortable with falling short of our goals, so our minds find it incomprehensible that we will soar and succeed. The tapes whir and click and clatter, filling the air with messages of negativity and dread.

"Call me if you need me," I say when we reach the lower level of the garage. "Have a good night."

Ben climbs into his car, fires the engine, drives away onto Mill Street. I follow him out of the garage in my truck, glance in the rearview mirror and realize another sweet, sweet miracle.

I'm smiling. For the first time today, a grin has appeared on my face. During the brief conversation with Ben, I've realized that being afraid is nothing to fear because it is an integral part of life. This understanding reminds me that I can get through anything with the love and support of my friends and the strength that now blossoms in my heart.

The ogres of insecurity, shame, and anger may continue to lurk in the distance, mirroring my movements and trying to undermine my progress. But I will no longer allow them to cross my path. I have my sense of direction. I know where I'm going and how I'll get there. And for the first time in my life, I have a traveling companion who shares my vision and values, a sense of humor and heartache, the wisdom of a kind word, the tenderness of a soft kiss.

I'm on my way. And I'm smiling. Miracles do happen. Dreams do come true.

———

And so I am home. Safe and certain that I've taken the best path in life, the path to sobriety. In the years before this moment, I spent endless nights wondering if I would ever reach a blissful destination. I wandered alone through the darkness. Staring into blank eyes and strolling through the bleak landscape, I never believed I could make the leap from the desperate place I inhabited to the serenity of my present world.

———

Find me. I will wait. Capture my heart. I will capture yours. Take this moment to tell me one secret. Breathe this life into your soul. Angels come when we are ready.

Find me.

———

"What are you doing tonight?" Sam asks when he calls in the early afternoon. "I woke up this morning and wanted my aunt's pasta sauce. So I've been cooking all morning. Would you like to come for dinner?"

I accept the invitation, spend the afternoon boating with Dave at Smithville Lake, debating the wisdom of buying a bouquet of flowers for Sam, thinking about how I will spend the night.

When I arrive at Sam's loft that evening, he's sitting outside the building with a neighbor, smoking and smiling.

"I'm just waiting for the other guys to arrive," he says. "They should be here in a few minutes."

"Oh," I say, wondering about the identity of the other guests. I put the flowers on the table and say, "These are for you."

I feel light-headed and clumsy and leaden. It's an uncomfortable feeling, and it will take a few weeks before I realize the source of the discomfort. I know that I'm searching for a mate, a partner, a best friend. I wonder if Sam is the one. He appears sincere and honest, yet there is a gentle hum just beneath the surface that sounds like a grenade's slow and threatening heartbeat. I spend a few days with Sam, trying to make him fit into the pattern of my life. He tells me he is also a recovered addict. He tells me he has been clean and sober for seven years. Sam tells me that after an insane period of crystal meth and casual sex in South Carolina, he moved to Kansas City to get clean.

The more we talk, the less I'm drawn to Sam. And the more I feel guilty. I'm engaged in double-speak; agreeing to see him for dinner or a movie yet knowing he is not the man of my dreams. On a lazy weekend in late October, Sam's behavior makes me increasingly uncomfortable. He's edgy and short-tempered, snapping sharp answers to my questions or ignoring my comments as we stroll through a small town north of Kansas City, window-shopping and browsing through the antique stores and linen shops.

In the end, the friendship with Sam ends in a muddy pool

of procrastination and fear. I struggle to find the words to tell him how I feel, yet they elude my grasp. I don't want to hurt his feelings, yet I find it impossible to be honest with him. Sobriety doesn't guarantee anything more than a clear head, an open heart, and the grace to handle the missteps that are a part of everyday life.

I regret how the friendship with Sam ends. I know that I failed to be honest with Sam because I listened to the old tapes. I was afraid to be truthful because I imagined that it would be perceived as bad news instead of honesty. By failing to be direct, I failed to be honest. It was a difficult lesson, one I had learned earlier in my recovery, one I may need to learn again in the future. I'm human. I make mistakes. I did the best I could to make amends and move on, and I hope that Sam will one day do the same.

———

A postcard written by Harrison, mailed in Paris: "Is there any way we deserve this beauty?" My reply, scrawled inside a Hallmark greeting card, mailed in Minneapolis: "Beauty fades. Truth is forever. I love you."

I have the postcard tucked inside a bureau drawer in my bedroom. It's a reminder that we all deserve beauty, yet we must never take anything for granted. I wish I could always remember the sweet reminders that life provides.

———

The constant click of anxiety's metronome in my head has been replaced with life's normal tension and conflict. There are moments of insecurity, periods of boredom, interludes of depression and anger and guilt. Regrets are few. Reason is firmly entrenched. Discipline and focus provide a foundation to support my interests, ideas, emotions.

I am not a saint or an angel. I fail. I fall short of my goals. I exceed my range and tumble to earth. There is pain and disappointment. And there is forgiveness and mercy and a strong heart that beats with hope and joy.

———

Look at this photograph, a group of four men seated at a table in a restaurant. We are at a café in the West Village, a restaurant I visit during each trip to New York. I'm sitting beside Jacob, a photographer I met on a shoot during my brief foray into commercial modeling. Ty and Joseph, a pair of pale creatures with a long and intertwined history of love and commerce, are turned in their seats, looking back at the camera over their shoulders. The waiter offered to take a picture at the end of our meal, a late-afternoon lunch on a Saturday in June.

"You guys look like you need to have a record of this lunch," the waiter suggested. "It looks like you're having such a fabulous time."

Fabulous. A word that has been trampled and soiled by modern gay men, British television actresses, and skeletal socialites with a hunger for only the best in life. I smiled at the waiter and accepted his offer to snap a picture, a permanent record of our meal, a frozen image of a time before Ty's life ended with an overdose of heroin on the floor of a hotel room in South Beach.

"He was experimenting," Joseph told me when he phoned from New York to give me the news. "He thought he could do drugs, any drugs. He couldn't have a fucking martini anymore, so he decided to experiment."

Sad results from a highly unscientific trial. Add another gravestone to those of the long line of men who fall victim to their fondness for self-medication and shame. Ty battled his disease for years. On some days, he was the king of

Columbus Avenue, beaming a bright smile at the world, in love with Joseph, proud of the design firm he founded, content with his friendships and his life. Other days, when the shadows wrapped around his shoulders, Ty was a tissue-paper man, expressionless face staring at the pavement, depressed about everything, convinced he was the biggest failure who had ever walked into an advertising agency to write copy for television spots about carpet cleaner, dog bones, and cruise-ship vacations.

"Experimenting can be good," I remember Joseph saying. "If you know what you're doing."

"That's the problem," I'd said. "If you know what you're doing, it's not experimenting."

"I know," Joseph had replied. "Ty thought he was bigger than the world. He thought he could have whatever he wanted without paying a price."

I remember the conversation, glance at the photograph, run my finger along Ty's handsome face. He was 28 when he died. He was a baby. A sad, tired, hungry baby. And not one person could comfort him.

I think about Ty's desperate heart, remembering my own sad times, the final four-day apocalypse in April so many years ago. The memories are sharp and clear, images broadcast from a moment just concluded, rather than a living hell that ended on the safe side of the horizon.

———

I wait for Riley to call, but he has disappeared. Again. I call his apartment one day and the landlord answers. He says that Beth is living in London and Riley moved away; there is no forwarding address. Just a U-Haul on a Thursday morning, a couple of trash bags left at the curb, no word where Riley may be today.

I hope he is safe. I also hope he is happy. Each damaged

spirit, every wounded heart, deserves to find a home in this world. I want to help Riley find the path that will lead him to a renewed understanding of his worth. I want to help him erect barriers to the fears and dark moods that ignite the desire to burn his soul to the ground with a long line of cosmopolitans and Cape Cods and gin martinis. I want to reach out to Riley and give him something to hold on to during the blinding white explosions of self-hatred.

I want to do these things for Riley. With his most recent disappearance, I can do nothing more than pray. And hope. I hope he is safe. I hope he is happy. And I hope he will call. Soon.

———

Quinn is on the phone, calling from a convenience store on Main Street. "I found a house," he screams. "Wait until you see it. You are going to die!"

I tell him we're all going to die one day. He fails to hear the humor in my remark.

"I'm coming over to get you," he says. "I can't wait to show you my new home."

The excitement in his voice is familiar. I too know the thrill of finding a new home, the physical embodiment of the dream. I feel this way about my sober self, the new home I've created to shelter my spirit, nurture my heart, and engage my mind. I know that each new home is a promise, a gift, a blessing. For years I ignored my spirit's cry for a home. I kept shuffling the cards, waiting for a better hand, imagining that someone else would handle life's loose ends, someone else would care about me and protect me from harm.

It takes nearly four decades until I have that someone, someone who matters, someone who cares.

It takes nearly four decades until I realize that the special someone was right here with me the entire time.

It takes nearly 40 years to discover that the special someone is me. I've become my own best friend, my own champion, my own beacon of hope and light. I can accept myself as I am at this moment. I know that I will continue to evolve, growing and learning with each new day. And now that I have my bearings and my compass is set for a happy, healthy, and sober destination, I look forward to the journey.

———

Angels arrive when we need them, when we are ready for miracles, when we are ready for dreams to come true. Some angels are messengers; others are guardians and guides. In the first three years of my new life, I meet many angels. Each is a blessing, an aspect of the miracle, a thread in the rope that connects hope to humanity, truth to integrity, wisdom to the heart.

———

Lou Jane is hosting a party in her loft for her daughter, the newspaper reporter from Atlanta. The gathering is on a Sunday night in early September. At the last minute, I decide to attend. Even though his hair is a mess and he has nothing to wear, Bill agrees to go. He's waiting in front of his apartment building when I arrive to pick him up, wearing white socks, shower thongs, black bicycle shorts and a hooded Eddie Bauer sweatshirt.

"Isn't this cute?" He points at a small pocket on the sweatshirt's left sleeve. "It's a little pocket for my cigarettes."

Perfect. Bill's a twisted mélange of *Men's Fitness, Vogue,* and "This Old Housewife." I can't help but laugh; he's a dear heart who has selflessly offered his love and support during the early years of my sobriety. He will always remain one of my favorite survivors; another of the walking wounded who finds a clear voice and a clean path to take him toward his destiny.

When we reach the party, two small children play on the stairs that lead from the street-level vestibule to the loft on the second floor. Upstairs, laughter and cigarette smoke blend with screams and the chatter of dozens of men and women, clustered around the room in small conversational knots.

I'm barely inside the room, my eye on the bartender and a bottle of club soda, when I turn and see Nan. She looks beautiful, her hair shorn and colored blond, her eyes rimmed with dark liner, her face a golden glow of cheery cheeks and red lips.

"Oh, my God!"

Our smiles explode when our eyes meet. Though I haven't seen Nan in months, I've heard she's managing a new Italian restaurant. I've been curious to hear about the job, her life, the state of her sobriety. When I returned to Kansas City in 1990, I waited tables while I built my freelance writing business. Nan was one of the kind professionals who gave me an opportunity to join the staff at a popular—and profitable—landmark restaurant. Though our paths have taken different directions in recent years, I'm still glad to see Nan and catch up with her stories and observations every few months.

"How are you?" Nan asks. "You look good."

I tell her I'm great. New job, new boyfriend, new attitude. Then I notice the glass of wine in her hand. I'm surprised. I'm curious. I'm also jealous. I would love to have a glass of wine, a glass of beer, a glass of vodka.

Nan notices me noticing her wine. "I think we should all just be in the place where we want to be," she says, a tone of dismissal in her voice. "That's what I think."

I'm surprised at the aggressiveness of her remark. I change the subject, we make empty conversation for a minute or two before drifting apart.

"I saw you talking to Nan," Gale says later. "I didn't think you were on good terms with her."

I smile and say, "There's no problem. I just haven't seen her in a long time. We were just catching up."

Gale pats my arm. "That's so nice to hear," she says. "I'm so glad you're doing so well. I used to worry about you, but now it looks like everything is OK."

I thank Gale for her kind words. I wander around, sample the food, sip a glass of apple juice. It's nice to be at a party and have a clear head. It's nice to know that in the morning, when the sun brightens the day and the promise of paradise awaits, I will have another happy memory of my clean, sober life.

An hour later, Bill and I leave the party. We chatter about the food, the loft, the other guests. Bill asks me about a man named Cody, a dessert chef with a reputation for creating edible art from chocolate and sugar. I ask Bill if he had a good time and thank him for joining me for the evening.

After I drop Bill at his apartment, I drive the dark night streets for a couple of hours. I think about Nan and her remark and the fact that it's been eight years since I met her and she appears to be back in a bad place. With her sad eyes and her pale skin, the glass of wine gripped tightly in one hand, I worry that she's drifting back into the dark. I go to bed later and say a prayer. For Nan. For Harrison. For Riley. I pray they will find peace, success, joy, and luck. I pray they will surface in the light. And I pray they will return to the sober circle and stay in its grace and power for good.

———

"How was your day?"

It's nearly midnight and Mike is calling from San Diego. He's on another business trip, five more days away from home. It has become a ritual to start and end each of our days apart with a telephone call.

"My day was marvelous," I say. "It started with you and it's going to end with you."

We talk about the events of the day, the business meetings and writing sessions, meals and conversations. Mike is in California to produce an event for a large corporation. He is a creative man, filled with vision and purpose, though his humble nature generally leads him to deflect praise.

During the late-night call, Mike and I share details and exchange questions. We laugh and whisper. It's like being a child again, a brave new spirit, a fresh expression of the unconditional love that can grow between two souls in search of the same peace, comfort, and joy.

"I love you," I say. "Thank you for being in my life."

"You are so welcome," Mike says. "I love you."

———

As the months pass, I make lists to document my progress. For anyone who returns to the real world from the bleak and frozen wasteland of addiction, it's crucial to celebrate the small steps, the incremental achievements, the progress and passions that illuminate the path along this journey.

The lists sit on top of the cabinet in the living room. I no longer date them, because there is no need for urgency. I don't need a string of words on a page to remind me about the important things in my life. Because the things that are important in my life are the things I do every day to nurture my heart, elevate my spirit, honor my soul.

———

I learn many lessons during the first years of sobriety. I learn to laugh with abandon, to love with passion, to contribute positive energy to the world. I learn to thank my friends for their friendship, to share my strength when it's needed by others, to move through each day with compassion, trust, and faith. I learn that I am at home in the world, that addiction and recovery were a part of my maturation process, one piece of the puzzle that would allow me to become the man I am today.

I am thankful for each moment. I treasure each day, every sunrise, the stars in the dark night sky. It sounds like a fairy tale, and in some ways my life has been like a fable from a child's storybook. With evil characters, winding plot twists, and wondrous miracles, the story of my life has been one remarkable journey for one common man.

I am not alone in the fable. There are thousands of men throughout the world who continue to struggle with alcoholism, who continue to labor beneath the stranglehold of their addictions. I pray they will experience their own miracles. I pray they will find a way to a sane, sober life. And I pray they will find the same simple joy that I have found by following my heart, trusting in the love and faith of my friends and family, and keeping my eye on the one simple word that made it possible for this miracle, this fable, this story to come true: Believe.

And I do.